THE ENCHANTED FEAST

A Romantasy Cookbook

GABRIELA LEON

HARVARD
COMMON
PRESS

Quarto.com

© 2025 Quarto Publishing Group USA Inc.
Text © 2025 Nancy Leon

First Published in 2025 by The Harvard Common Press,
an imprint of The Quarto Group,
100 Cummings Center, Suite 265-D, Beverly, MA 01915, USA.
T (978) 282-9590 F (978) 283-2742

All rights reserved. No part of this book may be
reproduced in any form without written permission of the
copyright owners. All images in this book have been reproduced
with the knowledge and prior consent of the artists concerned,
and no responsibility is accepted by producer, publisher, or printer
for any infringement of copyright or otherwise, arising from the
contents of this publication. Every effort has been made to ensure
that credits accurately comply with the information supplied.
We apologize for any inaccuracies that may have occurred
and will resolve inaccurate or missing information in
a subsequent reprinting of the book.

The Harvard Common Press titles are also available at
discount for retail, wholesale, promotional, and bulk purchase.
For details, contact the Special Sales Manager by email at
specialsales@quarto.com or by mail at The Quarto Group,
Attn: Special Sales Manager, 100 Cummings Center,
Suite 265-D, Beverly, MA 01915, USA.

29 28 27 26 25   1 2 3 4 5

ISBN: 978-0-7603-9651-3

Digital edition published in 2025
eISBN: 978-0-7603-9652-0

Library of Congress Cataloging-in-Publication Data available.

Design: Cindy Samargia Laun
Cover Image: Adobe Stock/Natalia Tan
Photography: Michelle Miller Photography
Adobe Stock Illustration: Natalia Tan, BigJoy, croisy, KOSIM, jenesesimre

Printed in China

For all lovers of romance and fantasy. May these dishes transport you to the magical world of your dreams.

Introduction: From Fantasy to Feast 7

CHAPTER 1

Breakfasts and Brunches Fit for Warriors and Dragons

Winter Solstice Ginger and Orange Pancakes 10
Breakfast Pull-Apart Bread 13
Brennan's Honeyed Biscuit Breakfast Sandwiches 15
Aelin's Mushroom Onion Scramble 19
Calanmai Pomegranate Shakshuka 20
A Warrior's Breakfast 23
Dragon Breakfast Bowl 24
Cadet Breakfast Sausage Rolls 27
Fairy Breakfast Savory Tart 28

CHAPTER 2

Appetizers and Party Food for Feasts, Fairs, and Festivals

Skull's Bay Spiced Prawns 32
Summer Court Ceviche 35
Violet's Foraged Stuffed Mushrooms 36
Fairy Charcuterie Board for Grazing 39
Dragon Wings: Calabrian Chili Chicken Wings 41
The 33rd's Cafeteria Finger Sandwiches 42
Lunathion Cedar-Smoked Grilled Cheeseburger Sliders 45
Savory Mini Meat Pies 46
Ruhn's Pizza: Pull-Apart Pizza Bread 49
The Court of Dreams Appetizer: Caprese Skewers 50

CHAPTER 3

Main Courses Worthy of the Finest Court

Mating Bond Lentil Soup 54
Cozy Beef Stew 57
Fairy Bowl: Spring Vegetable Buddha Bowl 58
Bryce's Chili Noodles 61
Wendell's Mushroom Melt 62
A Velaris Dinner: Lemon Verbena Swordfish 65
Feyre's First Fae Meal 66
Werewolf Bowl: Steak and Wild Rice 69
The Wing Leader's Pork Chop Meal 70
Autumn Equinox Pot Pie 73

CHAPTER 4

Drinks, Tonics, and Punches for Glasses, Goblets, and Bowls

Violet's Orange Creamsicle 76
Spiced Blood: Cranberry Sangria Punch 79
Blackberry and Bourbon Cauldron Punch 80
Faerie Wine Spritzer 83
Spicy Fantasy Margarita Pitcher 84
Almond Milk Chai Martini 87
Thimblet Latte with Orange and Cardamom Espresso 88
Spicy Molten Chocolate 91

CHAPTER 5

Faeries' Favorite Sweets, Treats, and Desserts

Starlight Jam Linzer Cookies 94
Jasmine Sugar Cookies 97
Feyre's Chocolate Cookie 98
Fonilee Berries: Hibiscus Truffles 101
Dragon Breath Spicy Chocolate Bark 102
Full Moon Black Sesame Pudding 105
Roses and Thorns Apple Tartlets 106
Xaden's Mint Chocolate Lava Cupcakes 109
Poe's Glazed Cakes 110
Quite Large Cinnamon Buns 113
Elaine's Garden Cake: Vanilla Lemon Brown Sugar
    Ice Cream Cake 115
The House's Double Chocolate Cake 119
The Valkyries' Sleepover Grazing Board 121

About the Author 124
Acknowledgments 124
Index 125

I came to be a fantasy romance fan in the same way that most of you did. I was in a reading rut and hadn't been able to find any books that made me feel excited. At the time, I was stuck in a job where I didn't feel appreciated and needed an escape. I craved to be transported to a fantasy world of make-believe.

Funnily enough, my therapist recommended I read *A Court of Thorns and Roses* by Sarah J. Maas. I ran to my local bookstore, bought a copy, and couldn't put it down. What ensued was a summer full of reading the first four books in the series as fast as I could. Through these books I discovered the entire romance fantasy genre and the expansive world of stories and series that exist out there. I fell in love with the characters, the scenery, the magical creatures, and the role that food played in the stories.

Whether intentional or not, food, or sometimes the lack of it, plays a huge role in the stories of many characters in fantasy books. At the beginning of many stories, characters don't have any food at all. They are hunting, fighting, and foraging their way through life for a few scraps of food. They vividly describe their stomach pains and weak bodies. Then they're transported to magical worlds where they get to try abundant and decadent food. In these magical lands, the food is able to bring people together. While eating, the characters often build connections or heal their emotions.

As a fervent foodie, I felt inspired to cook and bake some of the recipes described in these magical books. The first recipe I tried was a chocolate torte and I remember being nervous to post it. To my surprise, so many of you loved the video. Whether it's a birthday party, book club gathering, or other fantasy-themed celebration, people need fantasy cooking ideas. I hope that this book is able to give you inspiration for your next fantasy celebration, and for weekday and weekend meals as well.

Poe reappeared within the hour with a basket woven from willow boughs, covered with a coarse wool blanket. Bambleby accepted it ungraciously and without even glancing at the contents, even though whatever was beneath the wool steamed intriguingly. I had to take the basket away from him, and found within half a dozen glazed cakes, not unlike those I have seen Ljoslanders consume on special occasions. These would continue steaming until eaten.

—HEATHER FAWCETT,
Emily Wilde's Encyclopaedia of Faeries

Revolution tastes oddly . . . sweet. I stare at my older brother across a scarred wooden table in the enormous, busy kitchen of the fortress of Aretia and chew the honeyed biscuit he put on my plate. Damn, that's good. Really good.

—REBECCA YARROS,
Fourth Wing, Iron Flame

CHAPTER 1

Breakfasts and Brunches

FIT FOR WARRIORS AND DRAGONS

Winter Solstice Ginger and Orange Pancakes

In romantasy books, in the winter the characters tend to celebrate winter solstice rather than Christmas. They enjoy delectable breads, presents, and warm drinks. If you want to have a winter solstice brunch, enjoy these pancakes spiced with ginger and orange zest.

Serves 2

1 cup (120 g) pancake mix

1 teaspoon dried ground ginger

½ teaspoon ground cinnamon

½ teaspoon ground allspice

½ teaspoon baking soda

½ teaspoon salt

1½ teaspoons freshly grated orange zest

1 teaspoon vanilla extract

1 large egg

½ cup (120 ml) milk

Butter, for greasing

Fresh orange slices, for garnishing

Syrup, for serving

1. In a large bowl, combine the pancake mix, ginger, cinnamon, allspice, baking soda, salt, and orange zest. Use a fork or whisk to mix the dry ingredients together until fully incorporated.

2. In a small bowl, whisk together the vanilla extract, egg, and milk. Pour the egg mixture into the bowl with the dry ingredients and use a wooden spoon to stir the mixture together until no lumps remain.

3. Heat a large skillet over medium heat. Add in a small lump of butter. Once the butter is fully melted, add one-quarter of the mixture directly to the center of the pan, letting it naturally spread out into a circle. If needed, you can assist this process by picking up the pan and moving it in a circular motion.

4. Let cook until the top of the pancake has small bubbles, about 2 to 3 minutes. Flip the pancake using a spatula. Cook for another 2 minutes until evenly browned. Transfer to a plate.

5. Repeat steps 3 to 5 until all the pancake batter is used up.

6. Plate the pancakes by topping with fresh orange slices and syrup.

7. Enjoy!

Breakfast Pull-Apart Bread

If you're like me, one of your favorite things to discover while reading a romantasy book is what the characters are having for breakfast. Usually, it includes some sort of delicious bread, along with sweet treats and drinks. This breakfast bread is itself a sweet delectable treat, with the bread oozing with lemon curd and salted caramel.

Serves 4

Lemon Curd

2 teaspoons freshly grated lemon zest

½ cup (120 ml) lemon juice

2 large eggs

1 egg yolk

1 cup (200 g) granulated sugar

¼ cup (55 g) butter

Pull-Apart Bread

4 tablespoons (55 g) unsalted butter

1 loaf brioche bread

3 large eggs

¾ cup (180 ml) heavy cream

¾ cup (180 ml) whole milk

¼ cup (50 g) granulated sugar

2 teaspoons vanilla extract

½ cup (75 g) fresh blueberries

Salted Caramel Sauce

½ cup (100 g) granulated sugar

¼ cup (55 g) butter

¼ cup (60 ml) heavy cream, warmed

1 teaspoon salt

(recipe follows)

1. Preheat the oven to 350°F (180°C).

2. Make the lemon curd. In a small saucepan over low heat, whisk together the lemon zest, lemon juice, eggs, egg yolk, and sugar. Warm up the mixture very slowly until it thickens, about 10 to 15 minutes. Do not turn up the heat or stop whisking, as the eggs may curdle.

3. Remove the pot from the heat. If the lemon curd has lumps in it pass the mixture through a fine-mesh sieve. Stir in the butter.

4. Transfer the lemon curd mixture to a jar or bowl covered with plastic wrap and set aside to rest, cool, and continue thickening for a few hours. Once the lemon curd has cooled, you can begin to assemble the pull-apart bread.

5. Grease a loaf pan with butter.

6. Cut the bread into 8 slices, ½ inch (1 cm) thick.

7. Create 4 sandwiches by placing 1 tablespoon (20 g) of lemon curd on one slice of bread and setting another slice of bread on top.

8. Slice each sandwich diagonally and arrange them in the loaf tin, setting one crust side up, the next crust side down, and so on. Spread any remaining lemon curd over the top.

9. In a large bowl, whisk together the eggs, heavy cream, whole milk, granulated sugar, and vanilla extract.

10. Pour half of the egg mixture over the bread and let the bread soak up the liquid for about 10 minutes.

11. Sprinkle the blueberries onto the bread and finish pouring in the rest of the egg mixture. Depending on the size of the pan, there may be some mixture left over. That is okay; avoid overfilling the tin. Set the tin aside for 10 more minutes.

12. Bake for 25 to 30 minutes or until the eggs have fully set. Let the mixture rest for 10 to 15 minutes before serving.

13. Meanwhile, make the salted caramel. Sprinkle the sugar into an even layer in the bottom of a small saucepan over medium heat. Once the sugar begins to melt, begin whisking. You will have some clumping at this point. Continue whisking until all the sugar has melted and turned a deep amber brown color. Turn the heat to low and add in the butter. Continue whisking until the butter is melted. Remove the mixture from the heat.

14. Slowly whisk in the heavy cream and salt. Once combined, let cool slightly, then transfer the mixture to a jar.

15. Drizzle the salted caramel over the bread and serve. Enjoy!

Brennan's Honeyed Biscuit Breakfast Sandwiches

Violet eats honeyed biscuits in Rebecca Yarros's Iron Flame *as she heals from her war wounds. These breakfast sandwiches are inspired by the honeyed biscuits her brother Brennan serves her and are a sweet, savory, and hot mix of flavors. They are hearty breakfast sandwiches that will leave you and your guests feeling satisfied and ready for revolution.*

Makes 6 sandwiches

Hot Honey Biscuits

2 cups (250 g) all-purpose flour, plus more for dusting

1 teaspoon baking powder

1 cup (225 g) cold butter, cubed

⅔ cup (157 ml) milk

1 teaspoon salt

2 tablespoons (40 g) hot honey, plus 1 teaspoon

6 slices bacon

6 large eggs

2 tablespoons (28 g) butter, melted

6 slices cheddar cheese

1. Add the flour, baking powder, and cold butter to a large bowl. Using a pastry cutter, cut the ingredients until the butter is pea-size and a shaggy dough forms. If you use your hands, you run the risk of melting the butter.

2. At this point, create a well in the dough and add the milk, salt, and 2 tablespoons (40 g) of the hot honey to the well. Use your hands to mix the liquid into the flour mixture until it is well combined. Be careful not to overmix.

3. Lightly flour a surface and add the dough. Using your hands, flatten the dough into a rectangle and then fold one side towards the center of the dough. Take the other side and fold it over the top (like a brochure). Flatten this out and repeat the same folding procedure (this step helps create the flaky layers in the biscuits). Wrap the dough with plastic wrap and place it in the refrigerator for at least 30 minutes to let the dough and butter rest.

4. Preheat the oven to 375°F (190°C). Pull the dough out of the refrigerator and use a rolling pin to roll out the dough into a rectangle. The dough should be at least 1 inch (2.5 cm) thick. Using a large sharp knife, make one cut lengthwise, dividing the dough in half. Then position your knife vertically and cut through the dough twice. You should now have 6 biscuits.

(continued)

5. Arrange the biscuits on a baking sheet and bake for 20 minutes or until they are golden brown on top. Let the biscuits cool for 10 to 15 minutes.

6. Meanwhile, heat a medium skillet over medium heat. Add the bacon and cook until crispy, about 5 to 7 minutes. Transfer the bacon to a paper towel–lined plate. Do not discard the bacon grease. Leave the skillet over medium heat and add the eggs. Cook 1 to 2 minutes per side until the whites are set but the yolks are runny.

7. In a small bowl, stir together the melted butter and 1 teaspoon of hot honey. Stir until combined. Note: If this will be too spicy for you, use regular honey instead of hot honey.

8. Cut each biscuit in half and brush the insides with the butter and honey mixture. To one biscuit half, add an egg, a slice of bacon, and a slice of cheddar cheese. Place the top of the biscuit on top of the cheese and generously brush the top of the biscuit with the hot honey butter mixture. Repeat with the remaining ingredients until you have 6 sandwiches.

I sat at the table and studied the porridge and eggs and bacon—bacon. Again, such similar food to what we ate across the wall. I don't know why I'd expected otherwise. Alis poured me a cup of what looked and smelled like tea: full-bodied, aromatic tea, no doubt imported at great expense. Prythian and my adjoining homeland weren't exactly easy to reach. "What is this place?" I asked her quietly. "Where is this place?"

—SARAH J. MAAS, *A Court of Thorns and Roses*

Aelin's Mushroom Onion Scramble

Even assassins need breakfast and a sense of normalcy. In Queen of Shadows *(the fourth book in the* Throne of Glass *series), assassin Aelin prepares an egg and mushroom scramble while in her apartment with Rowan. It is a moment of escape from the chaos of the mission.*

Serves 4

8 large eggs

4 tablespoons (60 ml) milk

1 teaspoon salt

¼ teaspoon cayenne pepper

1 tablespoon butter (14 g) or oil (15 ml)

½ cup (80 g) diced onion

¼ cup (18 g) baby portabella mushrooms, sliced

¼ cup (30 g) shredded provolone or Swiss cheese (optional)

Bread, for serving (optional)

1. Add the eggs, milk, salt, and cayenne pepper to a large bowl. Whisk the ingredients together. Set aside.

2. Heat a large skillet over medium heat. Add the oil or butter and swirl to coat. Add the onion and mushrooms and cook, stirring frequently, for 3 minutes or until slightly softened.

3. Pour in the egg mixture and sprinkle with cheese (if using). Cook, undisturbed, for 1 minute or until the eggs are slightly set. Use a spatula to pull in the sides of the eggs to the center, letting the uncooked egg on the top spill out to the bottom. Repeat this step every 30 seconds until the eggs are just cooked, no more than 5 minutes total.

4. Serve with toast or bread, if you'd like.

Calanmai Pomegranate Shakshuka

In A Court of Thorns and Roses, the food for Calanmai, the Fire Night ceremony, takes two days to prepare. While this meal will not take you as long, it perfectly fits the Calanmai feast theme. The dish is a deep red color thanks to the runny yolk from the eggs and pomegranate and mirrors the sky in Prythian during Calanmai.

Serves 4 to 6

3 tablespoons (45 ml) olive oil

2 garlic cloves, minced

1 yellow onion, sliced

1 yellow bell pepper, diced

1 orange bell pepper, diced

¼ teaspoon ground cumin

½ teaspoon ground coriander

1 teaspoon smoked paprika

¼ teaspoon salt

¼ teaspoon pepper

1 (15-ounce [400 g]) can crushed tomatoes

4 Roma tomatoes

¼ cup (60 ml) pomegranate juice

6 large eggs

2 tablespoons (12 g) roughly chopped fresh mint leaves

¼ cup (44 g) fresh pomegranate arils, for garnish

1. Heat a large skillet over medium-high heat. Add the oil and swirl to coat. Add the garlic, onion, peppers, cumin, coriander, paprika, salt, and pepper.

2. Cook the vegetables, stirring frequently, for 5 to 8 minutes or until they are softened.

3. Reduce the heat to medium-low and add the canned tomatoes, fresh tomatoes, and pomegranate juice.

4. Bring to a simmer over medium-high heat, reduce the heat to low, cover, and cook for 15 minutes or until the sauce has slightly reduced.

5. Using a large wooden spoon, create 6 small wells in the sauce and 1 egg to each. Cover and simmer for another 5 minutes or until the egg whites are fully set but the yolks are runny. Remove from the heat and top with fresh mint and pomegranate arils.

A Warrior's Breakfast

Whether you're a cadet, an Illyrian warrior, an assassin, or a Valkyrie, a hearty and complete breakfast is important for staying ready and strong for any potential battle. Across fantasy worlds, we often find our main characters eating eggs, porridge, and sausages, all of which come together in this warrior's breakfast dish.

Serves 4 to 6

Side of Porridge

1½ cups (360 ml) 2% milk

¼ teaspoon ground nutmeg

½ teaspoon ground cinnamon

2 tablespoons (40 g) honey

Pinch of salt

1 teaspoon freshly grated orange zest

1 cup (156 g) old-fashioned oats

Main Breakfast

1 pint (340 g) cherry tomatoes on the vine

1 tablespoon (15 ml) olive oil

Salt and pepper, to taste

9 pork breakfast sausages

1 tablespoon (14 g) butter

6 large eggs

Side of Porridge

1. Add the milk to a small saucepan over medium heat. Add in the nutmeg, cinnamon, honey, salt, and orange zest. Stir until combined.

2. Bring to a simmer, stirring frequently. Add the oats and cook, stirring constantly, until the oats have absorbed all the milk, about 10 minutes.

Main Breakfast

1. Preheat an air fryer to 400°F (200°C). Add the tomatoes to the air fryer basket, drizzle with olive oil, and sprinkle with salt and pepper. Cook for 3 minutes. Add the sausages and cook until the tomatoes are roasted and the sausages are cooked through, about 7 more minutes.

2. Meanwhile, prepare the eggs. In a small skillet, melt 1 tablespoon of butter over medium heat. Crack the eggs directly into the skillet and season with salt. After 2 to 3 minutes or once most of the egg whites have set, reduce the heat to medium-low and cover the pan with a lid. Cook until the yolks have a slight white film (the yolks should still be runny). Uncover and transfer to a serving platter.

3. Add the tomatoes and sausages to the platter.

Dragon Breakfast Bowl

Dragon fruit is often a beautiful bright pink color, and it's almost hard to believe that it's a natural color. Similarly, the dragons described in Fourth Wing *are also vibrant and their scales are many different colors. This dragon fruit bowl is a nice and light breakfast that will have you feeling ready to soar high into the sky.*

Serves 2

2 (3½-ounce [100 g]) packages frozen dragon fruit smoothie blend

½ cup (90 g) diced fresh or frozen mango

2 tablespoons (40 g) honey

Pinch of salt

1 to 4 tablespoons (15 to 60 ml) milk (added as needed)

1 fresh dragon fruit, peeled and diced

1 fresh kiwi, peeled and sliced

¼ cup (25 g) granola

2 tablespoons (22 g) chia seeds

1 tablespoon (16 g) peanut butter

1 teaspoon sweetened flaked coconut

1 tablespoon (8 g) trail mix

1. Add the frozen dragon fruit, mango, honey, and salt to the base of a blender. Blend on high until smooth and thick, about 2 to 3 minutes. If needed, add in a few tablespoons of milk to smooth out the mixture.

2. Pour into two bowls. Divide the fresh dragon fruit, kiwi, chia seeds, nut butter, coconut flakes, and trail mix evenly between the 2 bowls.

3. Serve and enjoy!

POISONS

If there's anything we learned from Violet Sorrengail in *Fourth Wing* it is that a little bit of poison can, ahem, spice up your food. Poison is quite a big theme in many romantasy books. Various recipes in this book hint back to the many instances where characters may have added an extra something to a dish, including berries, mushrooms, and even a little bit of orange zest. Of course, in real life, we ask our guests if they have any food allergies or sensitivities before serving their food.

Cadet Breakfast Sausage Rolls

Protein is an important part of a warrior's diet. We see this in Fourth Wing *when the main character, Violet, starts the book losing her training matches. When two experienced cadets, Imogen and Xaden, take her under their wings, they encourage Violet to add protein (specifically breakfast sausages) to her fruit-only diet. Once she does, we see her body and strength improve significantly.*

Serves 4

1 (12-ounce [340 g]) package breakfast sausages

1 (17.3-ounce [490 g]) package frozen puff pastry sheets, thawed

All-purpose flour, for dusting

½ cup (60 g) cheddar cheese

1 large egg

Salt and pepper, to taste

1. Preheat the oven to 400°F (200°C).

2. In a large skillet set over medium-high heat, brown the breakfast sausages on all sides. They do not need to be fully cooked, as they will finish being baked in the oven.

3. Remove the sausages from the heat and set aside.

4. Roll out the pastry dough on a lightly floured surface.

5. Cut the dough into 4 rectangles that are the same width as the sausage.

6. Top each pastry dough rectangle with cheese and breakfast sausage.

7. Roll the dough around the sausage and the cheese tightly and place on a baking sheet lined with parchment paper. Repeat with the remaining dough and sausages.

8. In a small bowl, whisk the egg with a fork to create an egg wash. Brush over the tops of the dough. Sprinkle with salt and pepper.

9. Bake for about 15 to 20 minutes or until the dough is cooked through and golden brown.

10. Enjoy!

Fairy Breakfast Savory Tart

Breakfast tarts are a romantasy staple. Not only are they delicious, but they are also a beautiful breakfast table centerpiece. This breakfast recipe has the best ingredients for a rich and hearty tart. Decorate the top with edible flowers to create a fairy dream.

Serves 8

1 bunch of broccoli rabe, leaves removed

4 teaspoons (24 g) salt, divided

1 large red onion

1 tablespoon (15 ml) olive oil

1 (10-inch [25 cm]) frozen unbaked piecrust shell

6 large eggs

½ cup (120 ml) whole milk

1 teaspoon pepper

1 teaspoon paprika

4 slices deli ham

1 cup (115 g) sharp cheddar cheese

¼ cup (29 g) radishes, thinly sliced

1. Preheat the oven to 350°F (180°C).
2. Begin by preparing the vegetables for the filling. Bring a large pot of water to a boil over high heat. Fill a large bowl with ice and water and set it aside.
3. While the water boils, cut the broccoli into ½-inch (1 cm) pieces.
4. Once the water comes to a boil, add the broccoli rabe pieces and 2 teaspoons (12 g) salt and cook until bright green, about 3 to 4 minutes.
5. Immediately remove the broccoli from the boiling water and transfer it to the ice bath to cool for about 5 minutes. This step will preserve the bright green color and texture. Drain the water and set the broccoli aside.
6. Dice three-quarters of the red onion and reserve the quarter whole to use as a garnish.
7. Heat a small skillet over medium heat. Add the oil. Swirl to coat the pan and add the onion. Cook until softened, about 7 to 8 minutes. Set aside.
8. Add the piecrust to a pie plate. Prick the bottom of the piecrust with a fork and add pie weights. Bake the piecrust for about 10 minutes at 350°F (180°C). Remove from the oven and set aside. Remove the weights. Keep the oven set to 350°F (180°C).
9. Meanwhile, add the eggs, milk, 2 teaspoons (12 g) of the salt, pepper, and paprika to a large bowl. Whisk together vigorously until the ingredients are fully incorporated.
10. Add the sliced ham, cheddar cheese, broccoli, and red onions to the egg mixture and stir to combine. Pour the whole mixture into the piecrust.
11. Top with thinly sliced radishes and red onions.
12. Bake for 30 minutes or until the eggs are fully set.
13. Remove the tart from the oven and let it rest for 10 minutes.
14. Slice the tart into 8 pieces and enjoy.

CHAPTER 2

APPETIZERS AND PARTY FOOD

FOR FEASTS, FAIRS, AND FESTIVALS

Skull's Bay Spiced Prawns

In Empire of Storms, *Dorian and Rowan enjoy spiced prawns every night for dinner at their inn located in Skull's Bay. Enjoy these fresh prawns, seasoned with lime, cilantro, and red pepper flakes and enjoy with a side of rice.*

Serves 4

1 teaspoon freshly grated lime zest

1½ teaspoons freshly squeezed lime juice

2 tablespoons (2 g) chopped fresh cilantro leaves

1 teaspoon salt

1 teaspoon red pepper flakes

¼ teaspoon ground cumin

1 large garlic clove

2 tablespoons (30 ml) olive oil

1 pound (455 g) tail-on jumbo shrimp, peeled and deveined

Wooden skewers (soaked in water for 30 minutes) or metal skewers

1. In a large bowl, stir together the lime zest, lime juice, cilantro, salt, red pepper flakes, cumin, garlic, and olive oil. Add the shrimp and toss to coat. Cover and transfer to the refrigerator to marinate for 30 minutes to 1 hour.

2. Remove the shrimp from the marinade and thread 3 to 4 onto each skewer.

3. Heat a cast-iron skillet over high heat. Add the skewers and cook, undisturbed, for 3 to 5 minutes or until slightly charred. Flip and cook 3 to 4 more minutes, until evenly charred and cooked through.

4. Transfer to a large serving platter and garnish with fresh chopped cilantro and red pepper flakes. Enjoy!

Summer Court Ceviche

This white fish ceviche is a fresh appetizer that your book club guests can easily enjoy. In A Court of Mist and Fury, Feyre and Rhysand visit the Summer Court on a special mission to track down a magical book. This ceviche is inspired by the delicious seafood meal that they enjoy while secretly tracking down the invaluable book.

Serves 4 to 6

1 pound (907 g) white fish, such as cod or halibut

2 teaspoons salt, plus more to taste

Pepper, to taste

12 limes, juiced

1 red onion, thinly sliced

2 jalapeños, seeded and finely chopped

1 Roma tomato, finely chopped

⅔ cup (10 g) chopped fresh cilantro leaves

1. Pat the fish dry with paper towels. Season it liberally with salt and pepper and cut it into cubes ½ inch (1 cm) wide.

2. Transfer the fish to a medium bowl. Pour the lime juice over the fish (see Note). Allow the fish to rest, covered, in the refrigerator for 20 minutes.

3. Meanwhile, add 1 cup (240 ml) water and 2 teaspoons of salt to a medium bowl. Add the onion to the bowl. Let rest for 10 minutes. This helps soften the flavor of the onion so that it doesn't overpower some of the other ingredients. Drain the water and pat dry. Set aside.

4. Uncover the fish. It should be noticeably more opaque. If it is not, give it a stir, recover, and return to the refrigerator for 5 more minutes.

5. Add the red onion, jalapeños, tomato, and cilantro to the bowl with the fish. Stir until the ingredients are evenly distributed. Season with salt and pepper.

6. Serve with crackers or tortilla chips. Enjoy!

Note: The lime juice should cover the fish. If it does not, transfer the mixture to a smaller bowl.

Violet's Foraged Stuffed Mushrooms

Some mushrooms are sprinkled into eggs in the morning to make an opponent sick. Other mushrooms can be delightfully enjoyed and stuffed with cheese, butter, and onions. These small stuffed mushroom bites are bound to make guests want more.

Serves 6 to 8

2 cups (140 g) white mushrooms

2 tablespoons (30 ml) olive oil

1 teaspoon salt, plus more to taste

1 teaspoon pepper

4 tablespoons (55 g) butter

2 garlic cloves, minced

½ large white onion, finely diced

½ cup (60 g) plain breadcrumbs, plus more for sprinkling

⅔ cup (60 g) shredded Parmigiano-Reggiano, plus more for sprinkling

Pepper, to taste

1. Preheat the oven to 375°F (190°C).

2. Wash the mushrooms well, ensuring that all dirt and debris is cleaned. Remove the stems, dice them, and set them aside.

3. In a large bowl, toss the mushrooms with the oil, salt, and pepper. Set aside.

4. Melt the butter in a small saucepan over medium-high heat. Add the garlic and onions. Cook, stirring frequently, for 10 minutes or until the onions are completely softened.

5. Add in the breadcrumbs and the Parmigiano-Reggiano cheese. Stir until fully incorporated. Remove from the heat. Taste the mixture and add salt and pepper, if needed.

6. Line a sheet pan with parchment paper or foil. Arrange the mushrooms cut side up on the baking sheet. Using a spoon, stuff each mushroom with at least 1 teaspoon of the bread-crumb mixture. Sprinkle each stuffed mushroom with extra breadcrumbs and Parmigiano-Reggiano.

7. Bake for 15 to 20 minutes or until the tops are golden brown. Let the mushrooms cool for 10 minutes and serve. Enjoy!

Fairy Charcuterie Board for Grazing

This fairy charcuterie board is inspired by the various meals and stories of the main character, Feyre, in the series A Court of Thorns and Roses. *Whether it's an apple or a midnight chocolate cookie, snacking always plays an important role in keeping Feyre satiated. This charcuterie board is a nod to some of the snacks that Feyre has throughout her journey from human to fae.*

Serves 6 to 10

1 cup (225 g) cooked beets

¼ cup (38 g) goat cheese

Salt and pepper, to taste

1 Honeycrisp apple, sliced

1 bunch grapes on the vine

1 small loaf rustic bread, sliced

1 (9-ounce [255 g]) log salami, thinly sliced

3 ounces (85 g) prosciutto

1 (6-ounce [170 g]) package flatbread crackers

1 (8.5-ounce [250 g]) wheel Camembert cheese

1 (4-ounce [113 g]) log blueberry, lemon, and thyme goat cheese or similar berry-flavored goat cheese

1. Add the beets and the plain goat cheese to the base of a small blender. Sprinkle with salt and pepper. Blend on low until smooth and thick. Transfer the mixture to a small bowl and set on a large cutting board.

2. Add the apple, grapes, bread, salami, prosciutto, crackers, Camembert, and berry goat cheese to the board.

3. Serve and enjoy!

Dragon Wings: Calabrian Chili Chicken Wings

In Fourth Wing *we meet some incredible mythical creatures, including two dragons, Andarna and Tairn. These hot wings are a nod to Andarna and Tairn and their fiery personalities.*

Serves 4

Chicken Wings

1 pound (454 g) bone-in chicken wings

2 tablespoons (28 g) baking powder

2 teaspoons garlic powder

1 teaspoon salt

1 teaspoon pepper

Calabrian Chili Sauce

1 tablespoon (14 g) butter

2 garlic cloves, minced

¼ cup (85 g) honey

2 tablespoons (15 g) crushed Calabrian chili

1 teaspoon salt

Optional for serving: carrot sticks, celery, blue cheese dressing, ranch dressing

1. Preheat an air fryer to 350°F (180°C).

2. Pat the chicken dry using paper towels. Transfer the chicken to a large zip-top plastic bag. Add the baking powder, garlic powder, salt, and pepper.

3. Close the bag and shake until the chicken wings are evenly coated.

4. Transfer the wings to your air fryer basket. Arrange them in a single layer. You may need to work in batches. Cook for 10 minutes, flip, and cook for 10 more minutes until golden brown and cooked through.

5. Remove the chicken from the air fryer and let cool slightly. Meanwhile, heat a small saucepan over low heat and melt the 1 tablespoon (14 g) butter. Add the minced garlic and cook, stirring frequently, until fragrant, about 1 minute.

6. Next, add the honey, crushed Calabrian chili, and salt. Cook, stirring frequently, until the mixture thickens enough to coat the back of a spoon, about 5 minutes. Remove the saucepan from the heat.

7. Transfer the wings to a large bowl. Pour the chili sauce over top and toss to coat.

8. Increase the air fryer temperature to 400°F (200°C). Place the chicken wings back in the air fryer for 2 minutes. At this point, they should be a deeper golden color. If using, serve with carrot sticks and celery, as well as blue cheese or ranch dressing.

APPETIZERS AND PARTY FOOD

The 33rd's Cafeteria Finger Sandwiches

Cafeteria food isn't the most coveted in the world, but in House of Sky and Breath, *when Hunt and Isaiah meet up for lunch in the 33rd's cafeteria, Hunt's sandwich made my mouth water. The delicious combination of Brie cheese and turkey inspired these finger sandwiches with a sweet fig jam twist.*

Makes 18 small sandwiches

6 slices white bread

6 tablespoons (120 g) fig spread

Brie cheese, sliced

6 slices deli turkey

Salt, to taste

1. Place the bread on a cutting board and add 1 tablespoon (20 g) of fig spread to one side of each slice of bread. Top three of the six slices of bread with a layer of Brie cheese. Add the turkey on top of the Brie. Cover the sandwiches with the remaining bread with the spread side facing in.

2. Use a sharp knife to cut off the crusts on all four sides of each sandwich. Cut each sandwich lengthwise into three pieces.

Lunathion Cedar-Smoked Grilled Cheeseburger Sliders

In Sarah J. Maas's Crescent City series, Bryce is a foodie like the rest of us, and it's easy to understand when she lives in Lunathion with amazing restaurant options. After a particularly challenging day, Hunt gets Bryce some cheeseburgers as comfort food. These cheeseburgers are infused with cedar smoke as a nod to Hunt's cedar scent.

Makes 12 sandwiches

1 (15-inch [38 cm]) cedar plank

2 pounds (907 g) 80/20 beef

1 tablespoon (7 g) garlic powder

2 tablespoons (30 ml) Worcestershire sauce

Salt and pepper, to taste

12 slices American cheese

12 potato dinner rolls

Optional toppings: pickles, lettuce leaves, tomato slices, onion slices, ketchup, and mustard

1. Soak the cedar plank in water for at least 2 hours before using. This step will prevent the wood from burning on the grill.

2. While the cedar plank soaks, prepare the burger meat. In a large bowl, mix together the ground beef, garlic powder, Worcestershire sauce, salt, and pepper.

3. Separate the meat into 12 small balls and place them on a sheet pan. Cover and refrigerate for 10 to 15 minutes.

4. Preheat your grill to 375°F (190°C). Set the cedar plank directly on the grill grates.

5. Flatten the ground beef balls into ⅛-inch (3 mm) burgers and place on the cedar plank. Cook 3 to 5 minutes per side or until fully cooked. Top each with a slice of American cheese and continue cooking until melted, about 1 minute. Transfer the finished burgers to a clean parchment-lined sheet pan.

6. Place the buns sliced side down on the grill and cook until golden, about 2 minutes. Transfer to a clean plate.

7. To assemble: Add the burger patties to the bottoms of the potato rolls. Top with desired toppings and serve.

8. Serve with a side of your fries and chocolate shake.

Savory Mini Meat Pies

These mini meat pies are another quintessential item in any romantic fantasy dinner, whether as appetizers or as a side dish. The buttery crust and flaky top complement the saucy beef encased inside.

Makes 6 small pies

1 tablespoon (14 g) butter

½ pound (227 g) beef chuck, cut in small slices

1 tablespoon (10 g) finely chopped onion

1 garlic clove, finely chopped

Salt and pepper, to taste

3 tablespoons (42 g) butter, melted

2 tablespoons (16 g) all-purpose flour

1 cup (240 ml) beef broth

1 tablespoon (15 ml) Worcestershire sauce

1 tablespoon (15 ml) red cooking wine

Nonstick baking spray

1 (10-inch [25 cm]) frozen unbaked piecrust shell

1 puff pastry sheet, thawed

1 egg

1. Preheat the oven to 375°F (190°C)

2. In a large skillet over medium-high heat, melt the butter. Add the beef and cook, stirring frequently, until the juices of the beef release and have evaporated, about 5 minutes. Add the onion, garlic, salt, and pepper, and continue cooking, stirring often, for about 3 to 5 minutes. The meat will be browned on the outside but not fully cooked through.

3. Meanwhile, whisk the melted butter and flour together in a small bowl. Add the mixture to the skillet and cook, stirring constantly, for 30 seconds. Whisk in the broth, Worcestershire sauce, and wine.

4. Bring the meat and sauce to a simmer over medium-low heat and cook until slightly thickened, about 10 minutes. Taste and add more salt if needed. Remove from the heat and set aside.

5. Grease 6 compartments of a muffin pan with nonstick baking spray. Using a 4-inch (10 cm) round cookie cutter, cut out 6 circles of the piecrust. Cut a small line from the center of the circle to the outside. Place the piecrust into the bottom of each muffin tin. There should be an overhang of dough at the top. Using your fingers, push the dough down into the tin.

6. Using a spoon, evenly distribute the meat and sauce between the cups.

7. Using a 2-inch (5 cm) round cookie cutter cut out 6 circles of pastry dough. Place one pastry dough round on each of the mini pies. Using your fingers, pinch the piecrust and the pastry dough edges together, sealing the sides together.

8. With a knife, cut a small slit at the top of each pie dough; this will allow the steam to escape.

9. In a small bowl, whisk the egg. Lightly brush it on the edges of the piecrust. Bake for 15 to 20 minutes or until the dough is golden brown on top. Let the pies cool slightly before eating.

10. Remove the pies from the tin and enjoy!

Ruhn's Pizza: Pull-Apart Pizza Bread

In Sarah J. Maas's Crescent City series, pizza is practically its own character. This pull-apart pizza bread is inspired by Ruhn's pizza order, which is loaded with onion and sausage. While it may not be a proper pizza, it is just as cheesy, bready, and delicious as the real thing.

Serves 6 to 8

1 tablespoon (14 g) butter

½ large red onion, thinly sliced

1 pound (454 g) ground Italian sausage

1 loaf sourdough bread

2 cups (245 g) pizza sauce, divided

10 slices mozzarella cheese

5 fresh basil leaves

1 tablespoon (14 g) butter, melted

Salt and pepper, to taste

1 teaspoon Italian seasoning

1. In a small frying pan, melt the butter over medium heat. Add in the onions and cook until they have softened, about 10 minutes. Set them aside.

2. In the same frying pan, add the Italian sausage and stir frequently until the sausage is cooked through. Make sure that the sausage remains in large clumps as you would see on top of a pizza. Once cooked through, remove the meat from the heat and allow it to rest until it is cool enough to touch.

3. Using a large knife, begin to cut the bread—however, it should remain intact. Do not cut all the way through the bread; stop cutting about ½ inch (1 cm) away from the bottom of the bread. Then, take the knife and cut lines in the opposite direction with 1 inch (2.5 cm) of space in between. The lines should have created a square pattern on the bread.

4. Spoon 1 cup (240 ml) of the pizza sauce into the slits of the bread. Then, using your hand, grab the onions and push them down into the slits. Repeat the same step with the basil, the sausage, and the cheese. You will need to rip the cheese into smaller pieces to distribute it evenly in the loaf of bread.

5. Preheat the broiler.

6. Using a spoon or a brush, coat the top of the loaf with the melted butter, and then season with the salt, pepper, and Italian seasoning.

7. Bake for 10 minutes or until the bread is warmed through and the cheese is fully melted.

8. Serve and enjoy with a side of pizza sauce.

The Court of Dreams Appetizer: Caprese Skewers

In A Court of Mist and Fury, *Feyre has breakfast at the Moonstone Palace with the members of the Inner Circle and marvels at the beautiful platter of melon and tomato with light cheese, served with tea. These caprese skewers are a simple and light take on that meal and an easy appetizer for any party.*

Serves 8 to 10

15 cherry tomatoes

1 (12-ounce [340 g] container) marinated fresh mozzarella cheese, marinade reserved

½ teaspoon dried basil

¼ teaspoon red pepper flakes (optional)

¼ teaspoon dried oregano

¼ teaspoon garlic powder

Salt and pepper, to taste

15 toothpicks

Fresh basil leaves (optional)

1. In a medium bowl, combine the cherry tomatoes and 3 tablespoons (45 ml) of the marinade oil from the mozzarella. Add the dried basil, red pepper flakes (if using), oregano, garlic powder, salt, and pepper. Toss until well coated.

2. Thread one mozzarella ball onto a toothpick. Add a tomato and then another mozzarella ball. If you'd like, finish with a basil leaf. Then, add the skewer to a serving platter. Repeat with remaining ingredients.

CHAPTER 3

MAIN COURSES

WORTHY OF THE FINEST COURT

Mating Bond Lentil Soup

Listen, I get it. You're a busy person, and it'd be way easier to heat up a can of soup to solidify that mating bond like Feyre did. However, if you have a bit more time on your hands, you can make a delicious, simple, and hearty lentil soup that will strengthen any love bond that you have with your special someone.

Serves 4

3 tablespoons (45 ml) olive oil

3 garlic cloves, minced

1 small onion, diced

2 stalks celery, diced

½ teaspoon cumin

⅔ cup (120 g) wild rice

½ teaspoon salt

¼ teaspoon pepper

10 cups (2.4 L) chicken broth

1 pound (454 g) red lentils, rinsed and sorted

2 carrots, diced

Parmesan cheese (optional)

1. Heat the olive oil in a Dutch oven or large pot over low heat. Add the garlic, onion, celery, and cumin to the pot. Cook, stirring frequently, for 3 minutes or until the vegetables begin to soften. Add the rice, salt, and pepper. Cook, stirring frequently, for 2 more minutes. Add the broth, increase the heat to medium-high, and bring to a simmer. Cover, reduce the heat to medium-low, and cook 10 minutes.

2. Uncover the pot and add the lentils and the carrots.

3. Cover the pot again and simmer for another 30 minutes or until the carrots are softened and the lentils and rice are fully cooked through, stirring often.

4. Serve in a bowl topped with Parmesan cheese, if desired.

Cozy Beef Stew

If you're like Feyre and Rhysand from A Court of Thorns and Roses, *sometimes after a long day of traveling and training, you need to stop at a small, unassuming inn for dinner. This cozy beef stew is so comforting that it can warm you up even if you're drenched with wet clothes. The stew can be paired with a meat pie and a glass of red wine.*

Serves 4 to 6

2 pounds (908 g) beef chuck, trimmed and cut into 1-inch (2.5 cm) cubes

1 tablespoon (15 ml) Worcestershire sauce

1 tablespoon (3 g) fresh thyme leaves

Salt and pepper, to taste

2 tablespoons (30 ml) olive oil

½ large onion, chopped

1 garlic clove, minced

1 celery stalk

¼ cup (65 g) tomato paste

½ cup (120 ml) red wine

4 cups (950 ml) beef stock

4 rainbow carrots, sliced

1 parsnip, diced

1 cup (70 g) sliced portabella mushrooms

1 tablespoon (8 g) all-purpose flour

1. In a large bowl, combine the beef, Worcestershire sauce, thyme, salt, and pepper. Toss until well coated and set aside.

2. Heat a large pot over medium heat. Drizzle with olive oil and add the beef. Cook, stirring often, until brown on all sides, about 10 to 15 minutes. The beef does not need to be fully cooked at this point. Transfer the beef to a bowl and set aside. Don't turn off the heat.

3. If your pot is dry, drizzle with more olive oil. Add the onion and cook, stirring often, until softened, about 3 minutes. Add the garlic and celery and cook for 1 more minute. Lastly, add in the tomato paste and cook, stirring often, for 2 more minutes.

4. Add the meat to the pot and pour in the red wine and beef stock. Bring the stew to a simmer over medium-high heat and then reduce the heat to low and cover. Cook for about 40 minutes, stirring occasionally.

5. Add the carrots, parsnips, and mushrooms. At this point, taste the stew and season with more salt and pepper, if needed.

6. Whisk the flour into the pot. Cover and cook for another 20 minutes or until the beef is tender and cooked through.

Fairy Bowl: Spring Vegetable Buddha Bowl

In A Court of Thorns and Roses, *the first season of court we are introduced to is spring. Through the main character, Feyre, we are able to experience the colorful and abundant flowers in the Spring Court. This fairy bowl is inspired by the vibrant Spring Court. It uses colorful spring vegetables and is a perfect addition to a dinner party.*

Serves 4

1 cup (173 g) tricolor quinoa

Salt and pepper, to taste

5 radishes, sliced

½ cup (55 g) rainbow carrot ribbons

¼ cup (75 g) drained, quartered artichoke hearts from a can

¼ cup (28 g) roasted sliced almonds

Avocado slices (optional)

Dressing

¼ cup (60 ml) olive oil

1 tablespoon (15 ml) freshly squeezed lemon juice

1 tablespoon (20 g) honey

1 teaspoon Dijon mustard

Salt and pepper, to taste

1. Cook the tricolor quinoa according to the package instructions. Season with salt and pepper and set aside to cool.

2. In a small bowl, whisk together the olive oil, lemon juice, honey, Dijon mustard, salt, and pepper. Whisk until the texture thickens and the liquid turns a light-yellow color, about 1 to 2 minutes.

3. Divide the quinoa between 4 bowls. Top with the radishes, carrots, artichokes, sliced almonds, and avocado (if using). Drizzle with the olive oil–Dijon dressing. Toss and serve!

Bryce's Chili Noodles

In the Crescent City series, Lunathion has a host of incredible takeout food ranging from pastry shops to burgers to pizza and more. Bryce is no stranger to ordering out, and one of her favorites is chili noodles. These decadent noodles are easy to make and full of flavor just like the ones Bryce loves to eat.

Serves 4

16 ounces (454 g) pappardelle pasta

Salt

1 cup (235 ml) soy sauce, plus 1 tablespoon (15 ml)

2 tablespoons (26 g) granulated sugar

6 tablespoons (120 g) garlic chili crunch sauce

6 tablespoons (96 g) creamy peanut butter

2 tablespoons (30 ml) sesame oil

12 cloves garlic, minced

Sesame seeds

Red pepper flakes

1. Cook the pasta according to the package instructions, taking care to salt the water. Do not overcook the pasta.

2. Before draining the pasta, save about ¼ cup (60 ml) of the pasta water. Drain the pasta and set it aside.

3. In a small bowl, mix together the soy sauce, sugar, garlic chili sauce, and peanut butter.

4. Heat a large skillet over medium heat and add the sesame oil. Add the minced garlic and cook until it is fragrant, about 1 minute.

5. Reduce the heat to low. Add the peanut butter mixture to the skillet, stir vigorously, and cook until thickened, about 1 minute. Add the noodles and stir to combine. Add in the reserved pasta water, a little at a time, until the sauce is glossy.

6. Transfer the mixture to bowls and top with sesame seeds and red pepper flakes.

Wendell's Mushroom Melt

In Emily Wilde's Encyclopaedia of Faeries, Professor Wendell's mysterious origins are rumored to be in Ireland. The townsfolk give him a basket of mushrooms to enjoy as thanks for protecting them from some evil faeries. What could Wendell have made? Maybe he would have chosen a delicious mushroom melt and included the Iceland townfolk's bread, mushrooms, and some Irish cheese.

Serves 2

4 tablespoons (56 g) Irish butter, softened, plus 1 tablespoon (14 g), cold

4 slices sourdough bread

½ cup (80 g) thinly sliced onions

8 ounces (224 g) mushrooms, such as shiitake or oyster

Salt and pepper, to taste

½ cup (60 g) Irish cheddar, thinly sliced

1. Spread 1 tablespoon (14 g) of softened butter on one side of each slice of sourdough bread. Set aside.

2. Heat 1 tablespoon (14 g) of butter in a medium skillet over medium heat. Add in the onions and mushrooms and cook, stirring constantly, for about 5 minutes. Season with a pinch of salt and pepper. Once the mushrooms and onions are softened but still retain some of their texture, remove from the skillet and place in a bowl. Set aside. Reduce the heat to low. Place two slices of sourdough buttered side down in the skillet.

3. Onto the bread add one layer of cheese. Next, divide the entire mushroom mixture between the two cheese-covered pieces of bread. Cook for about 2 to 3 minutes or until the bottom of the bread is golden brown. Top with remaining two slices of bread, butter side up. Flip the sandwiches.

4. Cook the sandwiches for another 3 to 5 minutes. Using a spatula, gently press the sandwiches down into the pan.

5. Remove the sandwiches from the heat and cut in half.

6. Enjoy!

The faerie looked down at his hands, blushing and mumbling to himself. I reached into my backpack and drew out the remnants of Finn's burnt loaf. Sighing heavily, I broke it in half and began to chew. "That looks foul," the faerie said. He was beside me now, his long, long needle-fingers curved over the edge of a rock. I spat out a piece of the crust. "My host is a poor cook." "I'm a very good cook," the faerie said as soon as the sentence left my lips. I smothered a smile. Many of the common fae need little convincing to aid mortals and in fact enjoy the arrangement.

—HEATHER FAWCETT, *Emily Wilde's Encyclopaedia of Faeries*

A Velaris Dinner: Lemon Verbena Swordfish

This dish is an homage to Velaris in the series A Court of Thorns and Roses, *which is described as smelling of salt and lemon verbena. Fresh lemon verbena can be challenging to find in stores, so if you are not able to find it, you can use fresh lemon juice and lemon zest, as called for in this recipe. Either way, take in the herbaceous, salty, citrusy smells as you cook.*

Serves 2

1 pound (454 g) swordfish steak, skin removed (see Note)

1 tablespoon (18 g) salt, plus 1 teaspoon

¼ cup (60 ml) white wine

6 tablespoons (85 g) butter

3½ cups (100 g) baby spinach

2 teaspoons freshly grated lemon zest

1 tablespoon (15 ml) freshly squeezed lemon juice

1 tablespoon (3 g) fresh thyme leaves, plus more for garnish

1 teaspoon pepper

1. Pat the fish dry. Sprinkle the fish all over with 1 tablespoon (18 g) salt.

2. Bring the white wine to a simmer in a large saucepan over medium heat. Cook until slightly reduced, about 3 minutes. Add the butter, spinach, lemon zest, lemon juice, thyme, remaining salt, and pepper. Cook until the spinach is wilted, about 5 to 10 minutes. Remove the mixture from the heat and allow it to cool for 5 minutes.

3. Transfer the slightly cooled spinach mixture to a blender and blend on low for 1 minute or until smooth. Set aside.

4. Heat a large skillet over medium-high. Add 1 tablespoon (14 g) of butter to a pan and melt. Add the swordfish to the pan and cook, undisturbed, until golden brown, about 5 to 6 minutes. Flip and cook for 5 to 6 minutes more until both sides are fully brown.

5. To plate, pour half of the spinach sauce onto each plate. Place half of the swordfish on top. Sprinkle with fresh thyme and serve. Enjoy!

Note: If the swordfish comes in one large piece, cut it into two small pieces.

Feyre's First Fae Meal

This roast chicken dinner is an homage to the French-inspired Spring Court in the series A Court of Thorns and Roses *and the beautiful flowers described in the scenery. The herbed butter is flavored with lavender, adding a depth of flavor to the chicken. Enjoy this dinner with your favorite fae friends!*

Serves 4 to 6

1 (2½- to 3-pound [1.1 to 1.4 kg]) whole chicken, giblets removed

5 teaspoons (30 g) salt, divided

3 teaspoons (6 g) pepper, divided

4 tablespoons (55 g) unsalted butter, room temperature

2 tablespoons (6 g) dried lavender

3 sprigs fresh thyme

1 whole lemon, cut into 4 wedges

4 garlic cloves, whole and unpeeled

3 sprigs fresh rosemary

1 large carrot

1 large parsnip

3 white potatoes

1 large yellow onion, quartered

1 tablespoon (15 ml) olive oil

2 tablespoons (28 g) salted butter, melted

1. Preheat the oven to 375°F (180°C).

2. Season the chicken inside and out with 2 teaspoons salt and 1 teaspoon pepper.

3. Using one hand, gently lift the skin of the chicken and loosen it, without removing it. The skin should stay intact and connected to the chicken but should be lying on top of the meat.

4. In a small bowl, mix together the softened butter, lavender, 2 teaspoons of salt, 1 teaspoon of pepper, and the fresh thyme. Stir until a thick paste forms. Using your hands, rub half of the butter mixture under the loosened skin, directly onto the meat of the chicken. Spread the remaining butter mixture on top of the skin, taking care to ensure that the legs and wings are also buttered.

5. Place the quartered lemon, unpeeled garlic, and rosemary inside the chicken cavity. Set the chicken aside.

6. Cut the carrot and parsnips into half moons by cutting both in half lengthwise and then slicing into ¼-inch (6 mm) pieces. Next, cut each potato into 6 rounds.

7. Place the vegetables, including the onion, in the bottom of a roasting pan. Drizzle with olive oil and season with 1 teaspoon of salt and 1 teaspoon of pepper. Toss until evenly coated.

8. Set a roasting rack over the vegetables and put the chicken on top. If you want to prevent the wings from browning too quickly you can cover them with aluminum foil. Bake for 20 minutes. Brush the melted butter over the skin of the chicken. Return to the oven for 25 more minutes.

9. Remove the chicken from the oven, and let it rest briefly. Transfer the chicken to a large serving platter. Remove the lemon from the cavity. Squeeze the lemon over the vegetables. Toss the vegetables in the chicken drippings and lemon juice. Arrange the vegetables around the chicken.

10. Enjoy with a side of steamed asparagus and dinner rolls.

Werewolf Bowl: Steak and Wild Rice

The werewolves in romantasy books are often shape-shifters who run wild in the forests and aren't afraid to tear an enemy apart at all costs. The steak in this bowl is cooked to medium rare, and wild rice is an homage to the free feeling that they run with. The yummy garlic sauce will keep vampire enemies away and bring this meal together.

Serves 6

1½ cups (360 ml) water

2 tablespoons (36 g) salt, divided

2 teaspoons (6 g) garlic powder, divided

1 tablespoon (6 g) pepper, plus 1 teaspoon, divided

1 teaspoon turmeric

1 cup (160 g) long-grain wild rice

¼ cup (55 g) butter, plus 1 tablespoon (14 g)

2 pounds (907 g) New York strip or top sirloin (1 inch [2.5 cm] thick)

2 garlic cloves

3 cups (213 g) broccoli florets

¼ cup (55 g) butter

½ cup (68 g) raw unsalted cashews

⅓ cup (80 ml) milk

½ teaspoon paprika

1. Add the water, 1 teaspoon of the salt, 1 teaspoon of the garlic powder, ½ teaspoon of the pepper, the turmeric, and the wild rice to a medium pot. Bring to a boil over medium-high heat. Once the water is boiling, reduce the heat to low, cover, and cook for 45 minutes or until the rice is soft. Place 1 tablespoon (14 g) of butter on the top of the rice and let it melt in. Use a fork to fluff up the rice, cover, and set aside.

2. Season the steaks generously on each side with 1 tablespoon (14 g) of salt and 1 tablespoon (6 g) of pepper. Heat a large skillet (preferably cast iron) over medium-high heat. Place the steaks in the skillet and cook, undisturbed, until brown, about 6 minutes. Add in the garlic and ¼ cup (55 g) butter. Once the butter has melted, spoon it over the steak until the steak is evenly coated. Flip and repeat. Continue to baste with butter until the steak is done cooking, about 5 to 6 minutes for medium rare.

3. Fill a medium stock pot with 1 inch (2.5 cm) of water and bring it to a boil over medium-low heat. Place a steamer basket on the top of the pot, place the broccoli florets in it, and cover with a lid. Steam the broccoli for 8 to 10 minutes, until it is bright green and a fork can be easily inserted through a stem.

4. Transfer the steamed broccoli to a large mixing bowl. Add 1 teaspoon salt, ½ teaspoon pepper, and 1 tablespoon (14 g) butter. Toss until the butter is melted and distributed into the broccoli.

5. Add the cashews, milk, 1 teaspoon garlic powder, 1 teaspoon salt, and paprika to a blender. Blend on low until thick and smooth.

6. Slice the steak against the grain. Divide the rice between 6 bowls. Top each bowl with one-sixth of the steak. Add the broccoli on the side and drizzle each bowl with the cashew sauce. Enjoy.

The Wing Leader's Pork Chop Meal

During Violet and Xaden's sparring fights and encounters in Fourth Wing, *we learn that Xaden smells like mint. Like Xaden, this recipe is minty fresh. It's also packed with enough protein for any warrior to maintain her gains.*

Serves 4

4 bone-in pork chops

½ cup plus 1 teaspoon (125 ml) olive oil

1 garlic clove, minced

1½ teaspoons salt, divided

1 teaspoon pepper, divided

1 teaspoon smoked paprika

1 cup (96 g) finely chopped fresh mint

1 tablespoon (15 ml) freshly squeezed lime juice

1. Add the pork chops to a large bowl. Drizzle with 2 tablespoons (30 ml) oil and sprinkle with 1 teaspoon salt, ½ teaspoon pepper, and the smoked paprika. Mix the ingredients together until the pork chops are fully coated. Set aside.

2. Heat 1 tablespoon (15 ml) olive oil in a large skillet over medium heat. Add the pork chops and cook, undisturbed, until the skin is golden brown, about 3 to 5 minutes. Reduce the heat to low, flip the pork chops, cover, and cook for 5 to 6 more minutes. Transfer the finished pork chops to a serving platter or plates. Allow the pork chops to rest for 5 minutes.

3. As the pork chop rests, make the mint sauce. In a small bowl, whisk together the finely chopped mint, remaining olive oil, garlic, ½ teaspoon salt, ½ teaspoon pepper, and lime juice.

4. Pour the mint sauce over the pork chops and enjoy!

A long table-longer than any we'd ever possessed at our manor filled most of the space. It was laden with food and wine—so much food, some of it wafting tendrils of steam, that my mouth watered. At least it was familiar, and not some strange faerie delicacy: chicken, bread, peas, fish, asparagus, lamb . . . it could have been a feast at any mortal manor. Another surprise. The beast padded to the oversized chair at the head of the table. I lingered by the threshold, gazing at the food—all that hot, glorious food—that I couldn't eat. That was the first rule we were taught as children, usually in songs or chants: If misfortune forced you to keep company with a faerie, you never drank their wine, never ate their food.

—SARAH J. MAAS, *A Court of Thorns and Roses*

Autumn Equinox Pot Pie

Our fae and angelic fantasy friends celebrate quite a few holidays that are barely noted by humans, perhaps the most important one being the autumnal equinox. This pot pie is a nod to cozy autumn vegetables like acorn squash, carrots, and parsnips. To make it extra cozy, we tuck them under a crispy, buttery, and flaky crust.

Makes 1 (10-inch [25 cm]) pie

1 tablespoon (14 g) butter

½ large onion, diced

1 garlic clove, minced

2 carrots, diced

2 parsnips, diced

2 medium russet potatoes, diced

½ cup (70 g) peeled and diced acorn squash

Salt and pepper, to taste

¼ cup (31 g) all-purpose flour, plus more for dusting

1 cup (240 ml) vegetable broth

½ cup (120 ml) heavy cream

½ cup (120 ml) white wine

½ cup (65 g) frozen peas

1 sheet of pastry dough, thawed

1 large egg, whisked

1. Preheat the oven to 375°F (190°C).

2. In a large pot over medium heat, melt the butter. Add the onion and garlic and cook, stirring often, until softened, about 3 minutes. Add in the carrots, parsnips, potatoes, and squash. Cook until the vegetables are slightly tender, about 10 minutes.

3. Season the vegetables with salt and pepper. Stir in the flour until the vegetables are coated. Pour in the vegetable broth, stir, and cook for 2 to 3 minutes or until the broth has slightly reduced. Add the heavy cream. Cook for 2 minutes or until slightly reduced. Taste the mixture and add salt and pepper, if needed. Remove from the heat and set aside.

4. Transfer the vegetable mixture into a 10-inch (25 cm) pie plate.

5. On a lightly floured surface, roll out the pie dough until it is 10 inches (25 cm) in diameter. Set the dough over the vegetables and brush with the egg.

6. Bake for 15 minutes, until the pastry dough is puffed and golden.

7. After 15 minutes, if the center of the pastry dough needs to continue cooking, lower the oven temperature to 350°F (180°C) and continue baking for another 5 to 10 minutes.

CHAPTER 4

DRINKS, TONICS, AND PUNCHES

FOR GLASSES, GOBLETS, AND BOWLS

Violet's Orange Creamsicle

This creamy and citrusy drink is delicious on a hot night and will make you ready for any enemy that approaches.

Serves 1

¼ cup (35 g) vanilla ice cream

2 tablespoons (36 g) orange juice concentrate

¼ cup (60 ml) whole milk

1 tablespoon (15 ml) heavy cream

½ cup (70 g) ice

Whipped cream–flavored vodka (optional)

1 (12-ounce [355 ml]) can orange soda

1 orange-flavored popsicle or orange creamsicle

1. Add the ice cream, orange juice concentrate, milk, heavy cream, ice, and vodka (if using) to a blender and blend on high for 1 minute. At this point, it should have the texture of a milkshake.

2. Pour the mixture into a glass and top with orange soda. It will foam.

3. To garnish, add the popsicle.

ROMANTASY DRINKS

The drinks in romantasy books tend to get less attention than the elaborate dinners and meals that characters feast on. However, drinks can play a pivotal role in a storyline or character arc. Whether it's faerie wine that can completely inhibit a character, a medicinal tonic, a poisonous drink, or even bean water, drinks are vehicles to drive our favorite characters and stories forward.

Spiced Blood: Cranberry Sangria Punch

Many of our favorite romantasy characters need blood to survive, from Amren to Edward Cullen to Casteel. This is a "bloody" punch that all your guests can enjoy. It's spiced with cinnamon, allspice, and cloves. Disclaimer: No animals or humans were hurt in the making of the spiced blood punch.

Serves 6 to 8

1 bottle (750 ml) red wine

1 cup (240 ml) cranberry juice

3 ounces (84 ml) brandy

1 cinnamon stick

3 whole allspice

1 whole star anise

¼ cup (50 g) sugar or simple syrup

¼ cup (38 g) fresh or frozen cranberries

1 blood orange, sliced

8 ounces (235 ml) lime-flavored sparkling water

Ice (optional, see Note)

1. In a large pitcher, combine the red wine, cranberry juice, brandy, cinnamon, allspice, star anise, sugar or syrup, cranberries, and blood orange slices. Set the pitcher in the refrigerator for 2 hours to let the cranberries and spices fully infuse the wine.

2. Remove the pitcher from the refrigerator and discard the cinnamon stick and allspice.

3. To serve, pour the punch into a large punch bowl with a serving spoon. Pour in the sparkling water. Serve!

Note: If ice is needed, freeze one large block of ice. Smaller ice melts faster and will water down your sangria quickly.

Blackberry and Bourbon Cauldron Punch

Like calls to like, and this blackberry bourbon punch belongs in a cauldron-shaped punch bowl, if you can find one. If you can't, you can still enjoy this brew that packs a punch. The smokiness of the bourbon complements the tart blackberries and makes for a delicious drink to enjoy with friends. If you wish to get a dark color, add in black charcoal powder, which will significantly darken the color of the punch. You can also add edible glitter for a magical effect as well as some fresh blackberries.

Serves 6 to 8

Blackberry Simple Syrup

⅓ cup (50 g) fresh blackberries

⅓ cup (80 ml) water

⅓ cup (200 g) granulated sugar

Punch

2 cups (480 ml) bourbon

2 cups (480 ml) pomegranate juice or black cherry juice

1 cup (240 ml) blackberry simple syrup

2 cups (480 ml) sparkling water

Ice

Optional garnishes: extra blackberries, black edible glitter, or black charcoal powder

1. Begin by making the simple syrup. In a small saucepan, bring the water and sugar to a light boil over medium-high heat. Add the blackberries. Boil for 10 to 15 minutes or until the color of the syrup has significantly darkened and the liquid is slightly reduced. Remove from the heat and strain. Set aside to cool.

2. In a large pitcher or cauldron serving bowl, stir together the bourbon, juice, and cooled simple syrup. Garnish as desired and serve over ice.

Faerie Wine Spritzer

Faerie wine is a special drink to enjoy on a hot summer solstice day. Elderflower is one of the most common flavors that is associated with faeries, making it the perfect focal point for this faerie-inspired spritzer. This spritzer's delectable flavors and aroma will intoxicate you into playing the fiddle and dancing around a bonfire like no one is watching.

Serves 2

1 to 2 teaspoons
   blackberry jam

4 ounces (112 ml)
   elderflower liqueur

Ice

Edible glitter (optional)

6 ounces (168 ml) prosecco

2 ounces (56 ml) club soda

Optional garnishes:
   fresh blackberries
   or edible flowers

1. Fill a cocktail shaker with the blackberry jam, elderflower liqueur, ice, and glitter (if using). Shake until well chilled and the jam is evenly dispersed, about 15 to 30 seconds.

2. Divide the mixture between 2 glasses and top each with half of the prosecco and club soda.

3. Garnish with fresh blackberries or edible flowers, if using.

Then the food platters began pouring out, along with the wine and the conversation, and we dined under the stars beside the river. I'd never had such food— warm and rich and savory and spicy. Like it filled not only my stomach, but that lingering hole in my chest, too.

—SARAH J. MAAS, *A Court of Mist and Fury*

Spicy Fantasy Margarita Pitcher

This drink is an homage to the spicy romantasy genre. Margaritas are a great drink to enjoy for a romantasy book club meeting, but this recipe is spicy. The jalapeño simple syrup provides a warm heat that pairs well with the citrus. Enjoy with your book besties.

Serves 6

Jalapeño Simple Syrup

¼ cup (38 g) sugar

¼ cup (60 ml) water

2 tablespoons (18 g) sliced, deseeded jalapeños

Spicy Margarita Pitcher

¾ cup (180 ml) freshly squeezed orange juice

¾ cup (180 ml) freshly squeezed lime juice

1½ cups (360 ml) white tequila

¼ cup (60 ml) simple syrup

¼ cup (60 ml) jalapeño simple syrup

6 cups (840 g) ice

1. Begin by making the jalapeño simple syrup. In a small saucepan, bring the sugar and water to a boil over high heat. Reduce the heat to medium and cook 2 to 3 minutes. Transfer half of the mixture to a mason jar and set aside. Add the jalapeño to the pot with the remaining simple syrup. Reduce the heat to low and allow the mixture to simmer for 10 to 15 minutes. At this point, the color of the water will be slightly opaque and the liquid will slightly thicken. Transfer to a second mason jar and set aside.

2. In a large pitcher, stir together the orange juice, lime juice, tequila, plain simple syrup, and jalapeño simple syrup. If you are sensitive to spicy things, add in the jalapeño simple syrup last and gradually to make sure that it is not too overpowering.

3. Stir in the ice and serve.

Almond Milk Chai Martini

Step into Sarah J. Maas's cozy Crescent City with this Almond Milk Chai Martini. In the book, main character Juniper orders a similar drink, an almond milk chai latte, when meeting with Bryce. This cocktail is a yummy alcoholic twist on that drink.

Serves 4

½ cup (120 ml) water

4 tablespoons (60 g) instant chai latte powder

Ice

1 cup (240 ml) almond milk

6 ounces (177 ml) gin

2 ounces (59 ml) amaretto liqueur

3 ounces (89 ml) maple syrup

Optional garnishes: allspice, nutmeg, cardamom

1. In a small saucepan, bring the water to a boil over high heat. Whisk in the chai latte powder. Turn off the heat and allow the mixture to cool for 10 minutes.

2. Add the ice, cooled chai, almond milk, gin, amaretto liqueur, and maple syrup to a shaker and vigorously shake for 30 seconds. The liquid inside the shaker should be cold to the touch.

3. Pour into four chilled glasses, sprinkle with allspice, nutmeg, and cardamom (if using), and enjoy!

Thimblet Latte with Orange and Cardamom Espresso

In Travis Baldree's novel Legends and Lattes, *Thimble makes cardamom- and orange-flavored desserts called Thimblets. Those flavors also complement milky bean water (lattes) well, and so this is an orange and cardamom latte. The bitter espresso and sweet orange-cardamom syrup will warm you up on a chilly fall day.*

Serves 4

Orange and Cardamom Simple Syrup

1 cup (240 ml) water

1 cup (200 g) granulated sugar

2 tablespoons (14 g) freshly ground cardamom

1 tablespoon (6 g) freshly grated orange zest

Latte

4 to 8 tablespoons (60 to 120 ml) orange and cardamom simple syrup

2 cups (480 ml) whole milk, warmed

4 shots of espresso or 2 cups (480 ml) of coffee

Freshly grated orange zest, for garnish

1. In a small saucepan over medium-high heat, stir together the water and granulated sugar. Bring to a gentle boil. Add the freshly ground cardamom and orange zest. Simmer until thick enough to coat the back of a spoon, at least 10 minutes. Strain the mixture to remove the orange zest, leaving you just with the syrup. Allow the mixture to cool to room temperature.

2. Add 1 to 2 tablespoons (15 to 30 ml) simple syrup to a coffee mug, depending on how sweet you'd like your latte. Add 1 shot of espresso or ½ cup (120 ml) coffee. Use a spoon to stir the coffee and syrup until combined. Pour the warm milk over the coffee and finish with a pinch of orange zest.

Spicy Molten Chocolate

We are not all lucky like Feyre, who has an Alis who will bring her molten chocolate to warm her up. This is not your average hot chocolate. It is extremely rich and beautifully spiced. The cayenne pepper gives it a kick, and the fresh cinnamon whipped cream is the perfect topping.

Serves 2

Molten Chocolate

1 cup (240 ml) whole milk

¼ cup (60 ml) heavy cream

1 teaspoon brown sugar

¼ teaspoon cayenne pepper

½ cup (88 g) finely chopped 70% dark chocolate

Fresh Cinnamon Whipped Cream

½ cup (120 ml) heaving whipping cream

1 heaping tablespoon (6 g) powdered sugar

1 teaspoon vanilla extract

1 teaspoon ground cinnamon

1. In a small saucepan over low heat, add in the milk, ¼ cup (60 ml) heavy cream, brown sugar, and cayenne pepper.

2. Heat the milk for about 5 minutes. Do not allow the mixture to boil.

3. Remove the milk from the heat and add in the chopped chocolate. Vigorously whisk until the chocolate has melted and combined with the milk.

4. Allow the mixture to cool until it is a drinkable temperature.

5. Meanwhile, add the ½ cup (120 ml) whipping cream, powdered sugar, vanilla extract, and cinnamon to a large bowl.

6. Using a handheld mixer, whisk the liquid until stiff peaks form, about 3 to 4 minutes.

7. Divide the hot chocolate between 2 mugs. Spoon half of the whipped cream into each mug. Enjoy!

Though dinner was to be served soon, Alis had a cup of molten chocolate brought up and refused to do anything until I'd had a few sips. It was the best thing I'd ever tasted.

—SARAH J. MAAS, *A Court of Thorns and Roses*

CHAPTER 5

FAERIES' FAVORITE

SWEETS, TREATS, AND DESSERTS

Starlight Jam Linzer Cookies

In Crescent City, Bryce has an eight-point star birthmark that illuminates when she uses her starlight. These jam linzer cookies are as bright as starlight. Like the starlight symbol, the cookies are not only beautiful but bold.

Makes 6 large cookies

1½ cup (188 g) all-purpose flour, plus more for dusting

½ cup (96 g) almond flour

½ teaspoon salt

½ cup (112 g) butter, room temperature

½ cup (100 g) granulated sugar

½ teaspoon vanilla extract

¼ teaspoon almond extract

½ cup (160 g) fruit jam or hazelnut spread

1. In a large bowl, stir together the all-purpose flour, almond flour, and salt. Set aside.

2. In another large bowl, beat the butter, sugar, vanilla extract, and almond extract until creamy and smooth, about 3 minutes.

3. Add in the dry ingredients to the wet ingredients and beat on low until the flour is fully mixed into the dough.

4. Transfer the dough to a piece of plastic wrap. Cover and shape into a disk. Place this in the refrigerator for at least 30 minutes.

5. Preheat the oven to 350°F (180°C) and line a baking sheet with parchment paper.

6. On a floured surface, roll out the dough until it is ¼ inch (6 mm) thick. Use a lightly floured eight-point star cookie cutter to cut out 6 cookies. Using a smaller star-shaped cookie cutter, cut a small piece out of the center of half of the cookies.

7. Place the cookies on a baking sheet and bake for 12 to 15 minutes or until slightly golden at the edges. Allow the cookies to completely cool.

8. Once the cookies have cooled, take the cookies without the cutouts and spread a small layer of jam on each. Place a cutout cookie on top of each, lining the cookies up perfectly. Finish off each cookie by spooning an extra amount of jam into the cutout.

9. Serve and enjoy!

Jasmine Sugar Cookies

Some of the most captivating heroes in our favorite romantasy novels are winged heartthrobs. Whether our characters have Illyrian wings, demon wings, angel wings, or others, all wings bring a certain amount of magic to a story, just like these cookies. The sugar cookies are lightly flavored with jasmine adding a nice hint flavor and can be enjoyed with a nice warm glass of milk or tea. If you can find a wing-shaped cookie cutter, you can take these cookies to the next level!

Makes 12 cookies

Jasmine Sugar Cookies

4 teaspoons (12 g) dried jasmine (see Note)

½ cup (100 g) granulated sugar

½ cup (112 g) butter, room temperature

Pinch of salt

¼ cup (60 ml) brewed jasmine tea

1 large egg

1 teaspoon vanilla extract

1½ cups (188 g) all-purpose flour, plus more for dusting

Royal Icing

1 cup (86 g) powdered sugar

2 tablespoons (30 ml) milk

1 teaspoon vanilla extract

Food coloring

Edible glitter (optional)

1. Using a mortar and pestle, crush the jasmine.
2. In a small bowl, stir together the sugar and jasmine.
3. Beat together the butter and jasmine sugar with a hand or stand mixer until the butter has lightened in color and is fluffy.
4. Add the salt, 3 tablespoons (45 ml) of jasmine tea, the egg, and the vanilla to the bowl. Beat on low speed until just incorporated, about 30 seconds to 1 minute.
5. Slowly add the flour to the wet mixture while beating on a low speed. Beat until well incorporated.
6. Transfer the dough to a piece of plastic wrap. Cover and shape into a disk. Chill in the refrigerator for 1 hour. This step is essential; otherwise the dough will be too soft and the cookies will spread.
7. Preheat the oven to 350°F (180°C). Line a baking sheet with parchment paper.
8. Unwrap the dough and transfer to a generously floured surface.
9. Roll the dough until it is ¼ inch (6 mm) thick. Use a cookie cutter to cut out 12 cookies and set them on the prepared baking sheet with at least ½ inch (1 cm) of space between them.
10. Bake for 10 to 15 minutes or until the edges become lightly golden.
11. Allow the cookies to cool.
12. Meanwhile, make the royal icing. Combine the powdered sugar, milk, and vanilla extract in a small bowl. The consistency should be a thick but still runny paste. If using more than one color, separate the icing into separate bowls and add food coloring until you reach the desired hue.
13. Decorate the cookies with a thin layer of icing. Finish off the cookies with a light dusting of edible glitter, if using. Enjoy!

Note: The best place to find jasmine, since it's a specialty product, is online. If you can't locate jasmine, you can substitute dried lavender.

Feyre's Chocolate Cookies

The first book in the series A Court of Thorns and Roses *is a retelling of "Beauty and the Beast." One night, Feyre snuck out of her room and snatched a delicious chocolate cookie. These are chocolate sable cookies, the much cherished French cookies. Careful when eating and return to your room quickly, as a faerie king may try to stop you in the hallway.*

Makes 30 cookies

½ cup (112 g) butter, room temperature

⅔ cup (60 g) powdered sugar

1 teaspoon vanilla extract

1 cup (125 g) all-purpose flour

⅓ cup (29 g) Dutch process cocoa powder

½ teaspoon baking soda

½ teaspoon salt

3½ ounces (100 g) 70% dark chocolate, roughly chopped

Flaky salt or powdered sugar, for dusting (optional)

1. Beat together the butter, powdered sugar, and vanilla extract using a hand mixer or stand mixer set to a medium speed. Beat until the mixture becomes a pale yellow color, about 2 to 3 minutes. Do not forget to scrape down the sides of the bowl.

2. Add in the flour, cocoa powder, baking soda, and salt, and mix until all the ingredients are just incorporated. Gently stir the chopped chocolate pieces into the dough.

3. Transfer the dough to a piece of plastic wrap. Shape into a large log, about 10 inches (10 cm) wide and 1½ inches (3.5 cm) in diameter. Roll the log up tightly in the plastic wrap, folding the sides in like a burrito to hold the dough in. Place the dough in the fridge to cool for 2 to 3 hours.

4. Preheat the oven to 350°F (180°C). Line a baking sheet with parchment paper.

5. Use a sharp knife to cut the log into round cookie slices about ⅓ inch (8 mm) thick. You should have about 30 cookies.

6. Place the cookies on the prepared baking sheet with at least ½ inch (1 cm) of space between them. You will need to work in batches so as not to overcrowd the sheet. Bake each batch for 10 to 12 minutes or until the cookies look slightly cracked on top.

7. Allow the cookies to fully cool. If you'd like, sprinkle with flaky salt or powdered sugar. Enjoy!

Fonilee Berries: Hibiscus Truffles

Violet in Fourth Wing *is a master forger and picked these berries, called "fonilee" in the book, to poison people's food. Don't worry—these fonilee berries are not poisonous. But these truffles will stain your fingers, just like berries do.*

Makes 10 truffles

¼ cup (7 g) dried hibiscus flowers (see Note 1)

1 tablespoon (5 g) powdered sugar

¼ cup (60 ml) heavy cream

½ cup (87 g) 70% dark chocolate, finely chopped

1. Add the hibiscus flowers to a blender or food processor. Blend on low until the flowers become a powder. If there are larger bits of hibiscus, strain them out using a fine-mesh sieve.

2. Place the powdered hibiscus in a bowl and stir in the powdered sugar. Set aside.

3. In a small saucepan, warm the heavy cream over medium heat. Take care not to boil or burn the cream. Once the cream is warm (but not scalding), remove the pan from the heat and stir in the chocolate. Continue stirring until melted and incorporated.

4. Add 1 teaspoon of the hibiscus and powdered sugar mixture.

5. Place the chocolate mixture in a bowl and cover with plastic wrap. Place in the refrigerator at least 2 to 3 hours until set.

6. Use a spoon to scoop out and form small balls (see Note 2). Use the palms of your hands to smooth out the sides, if necessary.

7. Place a chocolate ball in the bowl with the hibiscus sugar powder and gently roll until evenly coated. Transfer to a piece of parchment paper. Repeat with the remaining truffles.

8. Enjoy!

Note 1: The best place to buy these is online.

Note 2: If the ganache is too hard to scoop, leave it at room temperature for 10 to 15 minutes.

Dragon Breath Spicy Chocolate Bark

This chocolate bark is an ode to Andarna's and Train's beautiful scales in Fourth Wing. *The dark chocolate and gold represent the beautiful friendship and kinship that these dragons share in the book. The chocolate is complemented with spicy nuts, which will give you a fiery breath just like your favorite dragons.*

Serves 4 to 5

½ cup (32 g) pepitas

1 teaspoon cayenne pepper

½ teaspoon salt

¼ cup (38 g) cranberries

¼ cup (28 g) chopped almonds

Gold edible glitter (optional)

10 ounces (283 g) dark chocolate melting wafers

10 ounces (283 g) white chocolate melting wafers

1. Add the pepitas to a small bowl. Sprinkle with the cayenne pepper and salt and stir until coated.

2. Line a sheet pan with parchment paper.

3. Spread the pepitas, cranberries, and chopped almonds in a single layer on the prepared sheet pan. If you are adding the glitter, it can be sprinkled over the entire sheet at this point. Set aside.

4. Add the dark chocolate to one microwave-safe bowl and the white chocolate to another. Microwave on high for 30 seconds. Stir. If the chocolate is not fully melted, microwave in additional 15-second increments, stirring each time, until it is melted.

5. Reserve 2 tablespoons (11 g) of each chocolate. Spread the remaining chocolate over the pepitas, cranberries, and almonds. Drizzle the reserved chocolate across the length of the tray creating a zigzagging pattern over the layer of chocolate.

6. Place the tray in the refrigerator and let the chocolate set for at least 1 hour.

7. Use the back of a wooden spoon to hit the center of the chocolate to fragment it into pieces. You may need to repeat this until the chocolate pieces are about the size of a graham cracker square.

8. Transfer to a serving platter and serve immediately.

Full Moon
Black Sesame Pudding

The Court of Nightmares in A Court of Mist and Fury *sounds like, well, a nightmare. It's dingy and dark. However, we learn this is only a decoy for the beautiful Velaris. This pudding is dark and gray because of the black sesame. Its exterior makes it undesirable for some, but if you give it a chance, the flavors are hidden in the sweet, thick, and rich sauce. Surprise your guests with this delicious pudding.*

Serves 4

½ cup (72 g) black sesame seeds, plus more for sprinkling

½ cup (75 g) unsalted dry roasted peanuts

3 egg yolks, beaten

½ cup (100 g) granulated sugar

1½ tablespoons (12 g) cornstarch

¾ cup (180 ml) milk

¾ cup (180 ml) heavy cream

¼ teaspoon salt

1. Grind the black sesame seeds and unsalted peanuts in a coffee grinder or blender set to high. At first, you will get a fine powder. Next a paste will form. Set aside.

2. Add the egg yolks to a large bowl and set aside.

3. Add the sugar, cornstarch, milk, heavy cream, and salt to a small saucepan set to medium heat. Bring the mixture to a simmer, stirring frequently. Then, remove the pan from the heat. Slowly whisk the mixture into the bowl with the eggs.

4. Return the mixture to the pot and turn the heat to low. Cook, stirring constantly, for 5 to 10 minutes or until it is pudding-like in consistency. Remove from the heat.

5. Whisk in the sesame seed and peanut paste.

6. Let the pudding cool slightly and serve with extra black sesame seeds on top. Enjoy!

FAERIES' FAVORITE

Roses and Thorns Apple Tartlets

An ode to the series A Court of Thorns and Roses, *which got me back into reading! These jammy apple tarts are the perfect treat. The only sugar in them comes from the jam and apple, so they aren't too sweet. Careful about biting into a pecan "thorn" while you eat them.*

Makes 4 small tartlets

1 cup (240 ml) water

1 tablespoon (15 ml) freshly squeezed lemon juice

1 red apple, such as Ambrosia, cored, seeded, and thinly sliced

All-purpose flour, for dusting

1 puff pastry sheet, thawed

5 teaspoons (33 g) strawberry jam

5 teaspoons (11 g) chopped pecans

Powdered sugar (optional)

1. Add the water, lemon juice, and apple slices to a microwave-safe bowl. Microwave on high for 1 minute. At this point, the apple slices should be translucent and bendable. If not, return them to the microwave until they are pliable. Pat dry with paper towels and set aside.

2. On a lightly floured surface, gently roll the dough into a rectangle that is roughly 12 inches (30 cm) long and 8 inches (20 cm) wide.

3. Using a sharp knife, cut the pastry dough into four long strips, each about 2 inches (5 cm) wide. Spread the strawberry jam across each of the strips, taking care to ensure even and full coverage. Sprinkle the pecans evenly over the jam.

4. Next, arrange the apple slices on one half of each of the strips. You should have several layers of apples, and the peels should be facing up.

5. Fold the bottom edge of the pastry dough over the filling. This should seal in the apple slices and the filling.

6. Gently roll the dough into a small bun. Press the edge of the dough to the side of the bun, ensuring that it is fully sealed. This will prevent the dough from unrolling during the baking process. Place the tart on a parchment-lined baking sheet. Repeat with the remaining three pastry strips.

7. Place the baking sheet with the tarts in the refrigerator. This step will keep the pastry dough cold.

8. Preheat the oven to 325°F (170°C).

9. Bake for about 15 minutes or until the tops of the pastries are golden brown.

10. Wait until fully cooled and sprinkle with powdered sugar, if desired.

Xaden's Mint Chocolate Lava Cupcakes

As Violet and Xaden get to know each other in Fourth Wing, *we learn one important fact about Xaden: His favorite food is chocolate cake. These cupcakes are dense, chocolaty, and minty, with a gooey molten chocolate center. Xaden would be sure to devour them in one sitting.*

Makes 6 cupcakes

½ cup (112 g) butter

3½ ounces (100 g) finely chopped dark chocolate

⅓ cup (42 g) all-purpose flour

½ teaspoon baking powder

¼ teaspoon salt

1 large egg

1 egg yolk

¼ cup (50 g) granulated sugar

½ teaspoon vanilla extract

¼ teaspoon peppermint extract

2 ounces (57 g) dark mint chocolate, coarsely chopped

Powdered sugar, for dusting

1. Preheat the oven to 325°F (170°C).

2. In a small saucepan, melt the butter over medium heat. Remove the pan from the heat. Whisk in the chocolate until well combined. Set aside.

3. In a large bowl, stir together the all-purpose flour, baking powder, and salt.

4. In another large bowl, beat together the egg, egg yolk, granulated sugar, vanilla extract, and peppermint extract, using an electric mixer set to high. Beat for 3 to 5 minutes, until the mixture has gained volume and become a light-yellow color. Continue to beat on low while adding in the melted chocolate. Beat on low until well combined. Next, add the flour mixture a little at a time.

5. Line a cupcake pan with cupcake liners. Spoon the batter into the cups until they are two-thirds of the way full. Place a piece of the mint chocolate in the center of each cupcake. Push the chocolate down until it is completely submerged.

6. Bake for 12 to 15 minutes or until the edges are set and the center is still slightly jiggly.

7. Allow the cupcakes to cool slightly. Sprinkle with powdered sugar and enjoy.

FAERIES' FAVORITE

Poe's Glazed Cakes

Emily Wilde often trades items with the brownie faerie in the forest in Emily Wilde's Encyclopaedia of Faeries. *Poe is a self-proclaimed amazing cook, and his favorite item to trade is warm, fresh bread and cake. On one occasion he gifts Emily glazed cakes. The flavor of these sweet cakes and the glaze are best enjoyed while exploring the faerie lands.*

Serves 6

Cake

½ cup (50 g) granulated sugar

½ egg

⅓ cup (80 ml) milk

1 teaspoon almond extract

1¼ cups (156 g) all-purpose flour, plus more for dusting

½ teaspoon baking powder

¼ cup (55 g) butter, melted

¼ cup (28 g) sliced almonds

Cake Glaze

1 cup (120 g) powdered sugar

1 tablespoon (15 ml) heavy cream

½ teaspoon almond extract

1. Preheat the oven to 325°F (170°C). Grease and flour 6 of the cups in cupcake pan and set aside.

2. In a large bowl, whisk together the sugar, egg, milk, and 1 teaspoon of almond extract. Stir in the 1¼ cups (156 g) flour and baking powder. Slowly whisk in the butter.

3. Spoon the batter into the prepared cups.

4. Bake for 15 to 20 minutes or until a toothpick comes out clean. Let the cakes cool completely before frosting.

5. In a medium bowl, whisk together the powdered sugar, heavy cream, and ½ teaspoon of almond extract. Mix the ingredients until the glaze is a thick runny consistency.

6. Pour the glaze over each of the almond cakes, letting the glaze fall over the sides of the cake. Sprinkle almond slices over the top of each cake.

7. Serve and enjoy!

FAERIE TRADING

A tip if you ever find yourself at a faerie door is that you can barter with the faerie if you think you have something valuable to trade! If you're lucky like Emily, you'll find a brownie faerie who will trade you many items for bread and other sweet confections. Sometimes, the breads have magical powers, like the ability to heal you or keep you warm even in freezing temperatures. These faeries and their trading customs can support you along the way on your travel adventures. If you aren't able to find a faerie to trade with, don't worry—there are a few recipes that you can use in this book.

THE ENCHANTED FEAST

Quite Large Cinnamon Buns

In Legends and Lattes, *the Ratkin Thimble has an incredible talent for making cozy sweet treats. These cinnamon buns are as big in flavor as Thimble's. Pair them with your favorite milky bean water (latte). They are decadent, cinnamony, and oh so moist.*

Serves 4

Dough

4 cups (500 g) all-purpose flour, plus more for dusting

½ cup (100 g) granulated sugar

1 teaspoon salt

2 (¼-ounce [7 g]) packets dry instant yeast

½ cup (120 ml) warm milk

½ cup (120 ml) melted butter

2 large eggs

Butter, for greasing

¼ cup (60 ml) heavy cream

Filling

1 cup (225 g) butter, room temperature

1 cup (225 g) dark brown sugar

½ cup (115 g) light brown sugar

1 teaspoon ground allspice

3 tablespoons (21 g) ground cinnamon

1 teaspoon vanilla extract

Frosting

2 cups (240 g) powdered sugar

1 teaspoon vanilla extract

3 tablespoons (45 ml) heavy cream

(recipe follows)

1. First, make the dough. In a large bowl, combine the all-purpose flour, granulated sugar, and salt. Stir until combined.

2. In a small bowl, gently whisk together the yeast and milk. Set aside.

3. Returning to the large bowl, begin to incorporate the wet ingredients. Using a stand mixer set to low, mix in the melted butter. Add in the milk-yeast mixture and continue to mix on low. Add in one egg at a time, waiting until each egg has been fully mixed in before adding the next.

4. Beat this mixture with a dough hook attachment for 7 minutes on high. After 7 minutes, the dough should be mostly smooth and not sticky. If the dough is excessively sticky, add in 1 tablespoon of flour.

5. Transfer the dough to a greased bowl and cover with a tea towel. Let rest for 15 to 20 minutes or until the dough has nearly doubled in size.

6. Meanwhile, prepare the filling. Use a stand mixer set to low to beat together the butter, dark brown sugar, light brown sugar, ground allspice, ground cinnamon, and vanilla extract.

7. Next, on a large lightly floured surface, roll out the dough with a rolling pin into a rectangle. The dough should be quite large, around 28 inches (71 cm) long and 14 inches (36 cm) wide.

8. Spread the prepared butter-sugar mixture on top of the dough, taking care to create an even layer.

9. Cut the buttered dough in half lengthwise to create two squares. Take one side of one square and roll it tightly onto itself. Cut the resulting roll into four separate rolls.

10. Divide the remaining dough into four evenly sized strips. Place one roll on its side on top of one of the strips. Wrap the strip around the outside of the roll. Set aside. Repeat this step with the remaining 3 rolls and strips.

11. Generously grease a 9 x 13-inch (23 x 33 cm) baking dish with butter. Place all 4 rolls in the baking dish and cover with greased plastic wrap. Allow the dough to rise for 1 hour.

12. Preheat the oven to 350°F (180°C) with a rack in the center position. Pour the ¼ cup (60 ml) heavy cream over the buns. Bake the cinnamon buns for 35 to 40 minutes or until the tops of the buns are golden brown and the centers are fully cooked through.

13. Prepare the frosting. In a medium bowl, stir together the powdered sugar, vanilla extract, and heavy cream. Mix until thick.

14. Once the buns are baked, remove them from the oven and let cool completely. Frost and serve!

Elaine's Garden Cake: Vanilla Lemon Brown Sugar Ice Cream Cake

We all have some hobbies that double as self-care. These hobbies often help center us during hard times. After Elaine becomes fae, in A Court of Wings and Ruin, *she finds solace in gardening at Rhy's townhouse. This ice cream cake is a symbol of the garden that Elaine grows as she is healing from her emotional wounds.*

Serves 6 to 8

Oil Pound Cake

½ teaspoon salt

2 teaspoons (8 g) baking powder

2 cups (250 g) all-purpose flour, plus more for dusting

¾ cup (180 ml) neutral oil, such as canola

1 cup (200 g) granulated sugar

½ cup (115 g) light brown sugar

3 large eggs

½ cup (120 ml) milk

1 tablespoon (15 ml) vanilla extract

1 teaspoon lemon extract

No-Churn Brown Sugar Ice Cream

1 (14-ounce [397 g]) can condensed milk

¼ cup (60 g) light brown sugar

¼ teaspoon salt

1½ cups (360 ml) heavy whipping cream

To Serve

12 lemon-flavored cookies, crushed

1 cup (240 ml) heavy whipping cream

2 tablespoons (10 g) cocoa powder

3 tablespoons (16 g) powdered sugar

½ cup (20 g) shredded dried coconut

Green food coloring

Edible flowers (optional)

(recipe follows)

FAERIES' FAVORITE

Oil Pound Cake

1. Preheat the oven to 350°F (180°C).

2. In a large bowl, stir together the salt, baking powder, and flour.

3. In another large bowl, whisk together the oil, granulated sugar, brown sugar, eggs, milk, vanilla extract, and lemon extract. Slowly add the flour mixture to the wet ingredients while continuously whisking. Stop mixing when the flour is fully incorporated.

4. Grease and flour a loaf pan and pour in the batter.

5. Bake for 35 minutes or until a toothpick inserted in the center comes out clean.

6. Remove from the oven and allow the cake to cool completely.

Ice Cream

1. In a small bowl, whisk together the condensed milk, light brown sugar, and salt. Mix together until the sugar has dissolved.

2. In a large bowl, whip the heavy cream using an electric mixer set to high. Once stiff peaks form, turn the mixer to low and slowly drizzle in the brown sugar and condensed milk mixture. Once combined, cover and store in the refrigerator.

To Assemble

1. Cut off the top dome of the pound cake and discard. Then, cut the cake horizontally in half, creating two even layers. Keep track of which piece is the bottom and which is the top.

2. Line the same loaf pan you used to bake the cake with a large piece of plastic wrap. The plastic wrap should hang out of the loaf pan.

3. Put the bottom piece of the cake into the pan. Pour the ice cream mixture on top. Place the crushed lemon cookies in a thick layer on top of the ice cream, then place the top cake layer on top. Secure the cake with the rest of the plastic wrap tightly, closing the pieces over top. Freeze for at least 8 hours.

To Decorate

1. In a large bowl, beat the heavy cream, cocoa powder, and powdered sugar on high until stiff peaks form.

2. In a small bowl, mix together the coconut and a few drops of green food coloring. This will be the grass for the cake.

3. Once the cake is fully frozen, tip it out upside down onto a plate or cutting board. Remove the plastic wrap.

4. Cover the top of the cake with a layer of chocolate whipped cream (this is the dirt). Then sprinkle with the green coconut (this is the grass). Layer with edible flowers, if using. Serve immediately!

The House's Double Chocolate Cake

In A Court of Silver Flames, *the House is an amazing character that tries its best to take care of Nesta while she is healing. It magically delivers warm soup and the most delicious double chocolate cake right to Nesta's door. This double chocolate cake is a rich and fresh take on that cake. It has a fudgy ganache filling and light mascarpone frosting.*

Makes 1 (9-inch [23 cm]) cake

Lemon Ganache Filling

7 ounces (198 g) dark chocolate, thinly chopped

¾ cup (180 ml) heavy cream

1 tablespoon (15 ml) lemon extract

Chocolate Cake

2 cups (250 g) all-purpose flour

2 cups (400 g) granulated sugar

¾ cup (65 g) cocoa powder

2 teaspoons (9 g) baking powder

½ teaspoon baking soda

½ teaspoon salt

1 cup (240 ml) whole milk

¾ cup (180 ml) canola oil

2 large eggs

2 teaspoons vanilla extract

1 cup (240 ml) hot strong coffee or water

Mascarpone Frosting

3½ ounces (100 g) dark chocolate, melted

1 (16-ounce [453 g]) container mascarpone cheese, room temperature

4 cups (344 g) powdered sugar

1 teaspoon vanilla extract

(recipe follows)

Nesta ate until she couldn't fit another morsel into her body, helping herself to thirds of the soup. The House seemed more than happy to oblige her, and had even offered her a slice of double-chocolate cake to finish. "Is this Cassian-approved?" She picked up the fork and smile at the moist, gleaming cake. "It certainly isn't," he said from the doorway, and Nesta whirled, scowling. He nodded toward the cake. "But eat up."

—SARAH J. MAAS,
   A Court of Silver Flames

FAERIES' FAVORITE

1. Preheat the oven to 350°F (180°C).

2. Make the lemon ganache filling. In a small microwave-safe bowl, combine the 7 ounces (198 g) dark chocolate and heavy cream. Microwave in 15-second increments until the cream and chocolate are incorporated. Stir between each increment. Gently stir in the lemon extract. Do not overmix or you risk curdling the ganache.

3. Make the cake. Line 2 (9-inch [23 cm]) cake pans with parchment paper.

4. In a large bowl, mix together the flour, sugar, cocoa powder, baking powder, baking soda, and salt.

5. In another bowl, whisk together the milk, oil, eggs, and vanilla extract.

6. Slowly sift the flour mixture into the wet ingredients. Add the hot coffee or water and beat with a hand mixer set to high until the batter is fully incorporated, at least 1 minute.

7. Distribute the batter evenly between the two cake pans.

8. Bake for 30 to 35 minutes or until a toothpick comes out clean from the center. Let the cake cool completely before assembling.

9. Make the frosting. Melt the 3½ ounces (100 g) chocolate in 15-second increments in the microwave, letting it sit between each increment.

10. In a large bowl, beat the mascarpone, powdered sugar, and vanilla extract on high until the sugar is fully incorporated, about 1 to 2 minutes.

11. With the mixer still on high, slowly drizzle in the melted chocolate and beat until combined.

12. To assemble the cake, level the cakes, if needed (by cutting off the tops). Place one of the cake rounds on a cake stand. Pour the ganache onto the cake and smooth it out until it is an even layer. Then, place the second cake round on top with the flattest side facing up.

13. Spread the frosting over the top of the cake and down the sides.

14. Serve and enjoy!

CHOCOLATE

It's astounding how many times chocolate desserts like torte, cake, and even hot chocolate are mentioned in romantasy books! Perhaps it's the fact that chocolate is sometimes said to be an aphrodisiac. Chocolate is an ingredient that is as decadent and rich as the stories we love consuming. I have tried to pay homage in this cookbook to the many chocolate recipes mentioned in my favorite romantasy novels.

The Valkyries' Sleepover Grazing Board

One of my favorite scenes in Sarah J. Maas's A Court of Silver Flames *is the sleepover that Nesta, Emory, and Gweyn have at the House of Wind. This grazing board has pieces of everything the girls enjoy that night, including the bubble baths (marshmallows), whipped cream with raspberries, and friendship bracelets. If you have enough supplies left over, leave some of the friendship bracelets out so that your guests can also make their own.*

Serves 8 to 12

Strawberries

½ cup (88 g) white chocolate chips

Green food coloring

1 pint (357 g) strawberries

Toadstool Pretzel Sticks

½ cup (88 g) white chocolate chips

Red food coloring

8 pretzel rods

White sprinkles

1 cup (45 g) mini marshmallows

⅓ cup (41 g) lightly salted pistachios

½ cup (40 g) vanilla wafer cookies

Frog shaped gummies or frog-shaped candy (optional)

Raspberry Whipped Cream

2 tablespoons (30 g) cream cheese

1 (8-ounce [225 g]) container frozen whipped topping, thawed

½ cup (65 g) raspberries

2 tablespoons (10 g) powdered sugar

Friendship Bracelets

8 red licorice laces

1 cup (weight varies) gummies with holes through the center

(recipe follows)

1. Make the strawberries. Add ½ cup (88 g) white chocolate to a microwave-safe bowl. Microwave in 15-second increments until melted. Add in 3 to 4 drops of green food coloring and stir until the chocolate becomes a matcha green.

2. Dunk a strawberry in the green-colored chocolate until it is almost completely submerged. Leave the top quarter and stem of the strawberry out of the chocolate. Pull the strawberry up and shake off any excess. Set the chocolate-covered strawberry on a sheet of parchment paper and let cool until the chocolate is solid, about 10 to 15 minutes. Repeat with remaining strawberries and chocolate.

3. Next, make the pretzel sticks. In a clean microwave-safe bowl, melt the other ½ cup (88 g) white chocolate. Microwave in 15-second increments until melted. This time, add in 2 to 3 drops of red food coloring and stir. The chocolate should be a crimson red. Dip a pretzel into the chocolate until it is halfway submerged. Remove the pretzel from the chocolate, shake off any excess, and set on a sheet of parchment paper. Cover with sprinkles and let cool until the chocolate has set, about 10 to 15 minutes. Repeat with remaining pretzels, chocolate, and sprinkles.

4. Make the raspberry whipped cream. Add the cream cheese, whipped topping, raspberries, and powdered sugar to the base of a blender. Blend on high until the raspberries are fully incorporated and the mixture is creamy and smooth, about 1 minute. Transfer the raspberry whipped cream to a serving bowl and set the bowl on a cutting board.

5. Make the friendship bracelets. Thread the gummies onto the licorice laces. Divide the candy evenly between the strings, taking care to alternate colors. Set the finished bracelets on the cutting board with the whipped cream.

6. Once the chocolate on the strawberries and pretzels has hardened, transfer both to the cutting board with the friendship bracelets and raspberry whipped cream.

7. Next, place mini marshmallows in a small bowl and add it to the board. Add the vanilla cookies to the board. Use the pistachios and frog candy to fill in any gaps on the board.

8. Guests can dip the marshmallows and cookies into the raspberry whipped cream.

9. Enjoy!

ABOUT THE AUTHOR

Gabriela Leon is a U.S.-born daughter of Central American immigrants with a professional background in community organizing, training, and nonprofits. A proud graduate of American University with a master's degree in public policy, Gaby has dedicated her career to empowering immigrant communities in the Washington, D.C. area. When she's not working to create systemic change, Gaby channels her creativity into the kitchen through her popular TikTok and Instagram channel, *HappyGabyCooking*. There, she blends her love of food, fantasy, and culture, sharing recipes inspired by her Latina heritage and romantasy worlds. Through every dish, Gaby transports her viewers to their favorite fantasy world, bringing a touch of magic to every video she makes.

ACKNOWLEDGMENTS

Writing this cookbook has been an adventure that I never in my wildest dreams thought I could make. Thank you so much to Quarto Publishing for giving me the opportunity to express my imagination and creativity in a new way.

To my family, whose Central American recipes and traditions taught me the magic of flavor and story from a young age. *Gracias a mi familia en los Estados Unidos, Guatemala y El Salvador por siempre apoyarme y enseñarme lo bonito y mágico dentro de nuestra cultura.*

To my close friends Susana, Matthew, Austin, Alison, Eric, Fidencio, and Elsi, who are the best taste testers and supporters I could have ever asked for. A special thank you to my mom for being my sous chef and most honest food critic. To all my romantasy cooking followers on TikTok and Instagram who have inspired me with your enthusiasm and supported my dream of blending fantasy and food. This would not have been possible without your support and viewership.

To the authors of the romantasy genre who inspired the magical worlds, creatures, and characters that these recipes are based on.

To the team at The Quarto Group, including the editors and photographers, for your patience and guidance throughout this entire process. A special thank you to Dan Rosenberg for reaching out and making this possible.

And, finally, to anyone who has ever lost themselves in the pages of a romantasy book: Thank you for letting this book be part of your magical world.

INDEX

Aelin's Mushroom Onion Scramble, 19
Allspice (whole), in Spiced Blood:
    Cranberry Sangria Punch, 79
Almond Milk Chai Martini, 87
Almonds
    Dragon Breath Spicy Chocolate Bark,
        102
    Fairy Bowl: Spring Vegetable Buddha
        Bowl, 58
    Poe's Glazed Cakes, 110
Amaretto liqueur, in Almond Milk Chai
    Martini, 87
American cheese, in Lunathion Cedar-
    Smoked Grilled Cheeseburger
    Sliders, 45
Apple(s)
    Fairy Charcuterie Board for Grazing,
        39
    Roses and Thorns Apple Tartlets, 106
Artichoke hearts, in Fairy Bowl: Spring
    Vegetable Buddha Bowl, 58
Autumn Equinox Pot Pie, 73
Avocado, in Fairy Bowl: Spring Vegetable
    Buddha Bowl, 58

Bacon, in Brennan's Honeyed Biscuit
    Breakfast Sandwiches, 15–16
Basil leaves
    The Court of Dreams Appetizer:
        Caprese Skewers, 50
    Ruhn's Pizza: Pull-Apart Pizza Bread,
        49
Beef
    Cozy Beef Stew, 57
    Lunathion Cedar-Smoked Grilled
        Cheeseburger Sliders, 45
    Savory Mini Meat Pies, 46
    Werewolf Bowl: Steak and Wild Rice,
        69
Beets, in Fairy Charcuterie Board for
    Grazing, 39
Bell pepper, in Calanmai Pomegranate
    Shakshuka, 20

Berries
    Blackberry and Bourbon Cauldron
        Punch, 80
    Faerie Wine Spritzer, 83
    The Valkyries' Sleepover Grazing
        Board, 121–122
Blackberry and Bourbon Cauldron
    Punch, 80
Blackberry jam, in Faerie Wine Spritzer,
    83
Black cherry juice, in Blackberry and
    Bourbon Cauldron Punch, 80
Bourbon, in Blackberry and Bourbon
    Cauldron Punch, 80
Brandy, in Spiced Blood: Cranberry
    Sangria Punch, 79
Bread(s). *See also* Sandwiches
    Breakfast Pull-Apart Bread, 13–14
    Ruhn's Pizza: Pull-Apart Pizza Bread,
        49
Breadcrumbs, in Violet's Foraged Stuffed
    Mushrooms, 36
Breakfast Pull-Apart Bread, 13–14
Brennan's Honeyed Biscuit Breakfast
    Sandwiches, 15–16
Brie cheese, in The 33rd's Cafeteria
    Finger Sandwiches, 42
Brioche bread, in Breakfast Pull-Apart
    Bread, 13–14
Broccoli
    Fairy Breakfast Savory Tart, 28
    Werewolf Bowl: Steak and Wild Rice,
        69
Bryce's Chili Noodles, 61

Cadet Breakfast Sausage Rolls, 27
Cakes. *See also* Cupcakes
    Elaine's Garden Cake: Vanilla Lemon
        Brown Sugar Ice Cream Cake,
        115–116
    Poe's Glazed Cakes, 110
Calabrian Chili Chicken Wings, 41
Calanmai Pomegranate Shakshuka, 20

Caprese Skewers, 50
Caramel sauce, in Breakfast Pull-Apart
    Bread, 13–14
Cardamom, in Thimblet Latte with
    Orange and Cardamom Espresso, 88
Carrots
    Autumn Equinox Pot Pie, 73
    Cozy Beef Stew, 57
    Dragon Wings: Calabrian Chili
        Chicken Wings, 41
    Fairy Bowl: Spring Vegetable Buddha
        Bowl, 58
    Feyre's First Fae Meal, 66
    Mating Bond Lentil Soup, 54
Cayenne pepper
    Aelin's Mushroom Onion Scramble, 19
    Dragon Breath Spicy Chocolate Bark,
        102
    Spicy Molten Chocolate, 91
Ceviche, Summer Court, 35
Chai latte powder, in Almond Milk Chai
    Martini, 87
Charcuterie Board for Grazing, 39
Cheddar cheese
    Brennan's Honeyed Biscuit Breakfast
        Sandwiches, 15–16
    Cadet Breakfast Sausage Rolls, 27
    Fairy Breakfast Savory Tart, 28
    Wendell's Mushroom Melt, 62
Cheese. *See also* Cheddar cheese
    Aelin's Mushroom Onion Scramble, 19
    The Court of Dreams Appetizer:
        Caprese Skewers, 50
    Fairy Charcuterie Board for Grazing, 39
    Lunathion Cedar-Smoked Grilled
        Cheeseburger Sliders, 45
    Mating Bond Lentil Soup, 54
    Ruhn's Pizza: Pull-Apart Pizza Bread,
        49
    The 33rd's Cafeteria Finger Sandwiches,
        42
    Violet's Foraged Stuffed Mushrooms,
        36

125

Cherry tomatoes
  The Court of Dreams Appetizer:
    Caprese Skewers, 50
  A Warrior's Breakfast, 23
Chicken
  Dragon Wings: Calabrian Chili
    Chicken Wings, 41
  Feyre's First Fae Meal, 66
Chicken broth, in Mating Bond Lentil
    Soup, 54
Chili crunch sauce, in Bryce's Chili
    Noodles, 61
Chocolate
  Dragon Breath Spicy Chocolate Bark,
    102
  Feyre's Chocolate Cookies, 98
  Fonilee Berries: Hibiscus Truffles, 101
  The House's Double Chocolate Cake,
    119–120
  Spicy Molten Chocolate, 91
  The Valkyries' Sleepover Grazing
    Board, 121–122
  Xaden's Mint Chocolate Lava
    Cupcakes, 109
Cilantro
  Skull's Bay Spiced Prawns, 32
  Summer Court Ceviche, 35
Cinnamon Buns, Quite Large, 113–114
Cinnamon stick, in Spiced Blood:
    Cranberry Sangria Punch, 79
Club soda, in Faerie Wine Spritzer, 83
Cocoa powder
  Elaine's Garden Cake: Vanilla Lemon
    Brown Sugar Ice Cream Cake,
    115–116
  Feyre's Chocolate Cookie, 98
  The House's Double Chocolate Cake,
    119–120
Coconut
  Dragon Breakfast Bowl, 24
  Elaine's Garden Cake: Vanilla Lemon
    Brown Sugar Ice Cream Cake,
    115–116
Coffee
  The House's Double Chocolate Cake,
    119–120
  Thimblet Latte with Orange and
    Cardamom Espresso, 88

Cookies
  Elaine's Garden Cake: Vanilla Lemon
    Brown Sugar Ice Cream Cake,
    115–116
  Jasmine Sugar Cookies, 97
  Feyre's Chocolate Cookies, 98
  Starlight Jam Linzer Cookies, 94
The Court of Dreams Appetizer: Caprese
    Skewers, 50
A Court of Mist and Fury (Maas), 35, 50,
    105
A Court of Thorns and Roses (Maas), 7,
    20, 39, 57, 58, 65, 66, 98, 106
Cozy Beef Stew, 57
Crackers, in Fairy Charcuterie Board for
    Grazing, 39
Cranberries/cranberry juice
  Dragon Breath Spicy Chocolate Bark,
    102
  Spiced Blood: Cranberry Sangria
    Punch, 79
Cream cheese, in The Valkyries'
    Sleepover Grazing Board, 121–122
Crescent City (Maas), 45, 49, 61, 87, 94
Cupcakes
  Poe's Glazed Cakes, 110
  Xaden's Mint Chocolate Lava
    Cupcakes, 109

Deli meat
  The 33rd's Cafeteria Finger Sandwiches,
    42
  Fairy Breakfast Savory Tart, 28
Dragon Breakfast Bowl, 24
Dragon Breath Spicy Chocolate Bark, 102
Dragon fruit, in Dragon Breakfast Bowl,
    24
Dragon Wings: Calabrian Chili Chicken
    Wings, 41

Edible glitter
  Dragon Breath Spicy Chocolate Bark,
    102
  Faerie Wine Spritzer, 83
  Jasmine Sugar Cookies, 97
Eggs
  Aelin's Mushroom Onion Scramble, 19
  Breakfast Pull-Apart Bread, 13–14

Brennan's Honeyed Biscuit Breakfast
    Sandwiches, 15–16
Cadet Breakfast Sausage Rolls, 27
Calanmai Pomegranate Shakshuka, 20
Fairy Breakfast Savory Tart, 28
A Warrior's Breakfast, 23
Elaine's Garden Cake: Vanilla Lemon
    Brown Sugar Ice Cream Cake,
    115–116
Elderflower liqueur, in Faerie Wine
    Spritzer, 83
Emily Wilde's Encyclopaedia of Faeries
    (Fawcett), 7, 62, 110
Empire of Storms (Maas), 32
Espresso, in Thimblet Latte with Orange
    and Cardamom Espresso, 88

Faerie trading, 110
Faerie Wine Spritzer, 83
Fairy Bowl: Spring Vegetable Buddha
    Bowl, 58
Fairy Breakfast Savory Tart, 28
Fairy Charcuterie Board for Grazing, 39
Jasmine Sugar Cookies, 97
Feyre's Chocolate Cookies, 98
Feyre's First Fae Meal, 66
Fig spread, in The 33rd's Cafeteria Finger
    Sandwiches, 42
Fish and seafood
  Skull's Bay Spiced Prawns, 32
  Summer Court Ceviche, 35
  A Velaris Dinner: Lemon Verbena
    Swordfish, 65
Fonilee Berries: Hibiscus Truffles, 101
Fourth Wing (Yarros), 24, 41
Fruit jam
  Faerie Wine Spritzer, 83
  Roses and Thorns Apple Tartlets, 106
  Starlight Jam Linzer Cookies, 94
Full Moon Black Sesame Pudding, 105

Lemon Ganache Filling, in The House's
    Double Chocolate Cake, 119–120
Gin, in Almond Milk Chai Martini, 87
Glitter. *See* Edible glitter
Goat cheese, in Fairy Charcuterie Board
    for Grazing, 39
Granola, in Dragon Breakfast Bowl, 24

Grapes, in Fairy Charcuterie Board for Grazing, 39
Gummies, in The Valkyries' Sleepover Grazing Board, 121–122

Ham, in Fairy Breakfast Savory Tart, 28
Hazelnut spread, in Starlight Jam Linzer Cookies, 94
Heavy cream
　Autumn Equinox Pot Pie, 73
　Breakfast Pull-Apart Bread, 13–14
　Elaine's Garden Cake: Vanilla Lemon Brown Sugar Ice Cream Cake, 115–116
　Fonilee Berries: Hibiscus Truffles, 101
　Full Moon Black Sesame Pudding, 105
　The House's Double Chocolate Cake, 119–120
　Poe's Glazed Cakes, 110
　Quite Large Cinnamon Buns, 113–114
　Spicy Molten Chocolate, 91
　Violet's Orange Creamsicle, 76
House of Sky and Breath (Maas), 42
The House's Double Chocolate Cake, 119–120

Ice cream
　Elaine's Garden Cake: Vanilla Lemon Brown Sugar Ice Cream Cake, 115–116
　Violet's Orange Creamsicle, 76
Iron Flame (Yarros), 15

Jalapeño
　Spicy Fantasy Margarita Pitcher, 84
　Summer Court Ceviche, 35
Jam. *See* Fruit jam
Jasmine, in Jasmine Sugar Cookies, 97

Lavender, in Feyre's First Fae Meal, 66
Legends and Lattes (Baldrees), 88, 113
Lemon
　Breakfast Pull-Apart Bread, 13–14
　Elaine's Garden Cake: Vanilla Lemon Brown Sugar Ice Cream Cake, 115–116
　Feyre's First Fae Meal, 66

The House's Double Chocolate Cake, 119–120
A Velaris Dinner: Lemon Verbena Swordfish, 65
Lentils, in Mating Bond Lentil Soup, 54
Licorice, in The Valkyries' Sleepover Grazing Board, 121–122
Limes
　Skull's Bay Spiced Prawns, 32
　Spicy Fantasy Margarita Pitcher, 84
　Summer Court Ceviche, 35
Lunathion Cedar-Smoked Grilled Cheeseburger Sliders, 45

Maas, Sarah J., 7. *See also* Book titles/series by Sarah J. Maas
Mango, in Dragon Breakfast Bowl, 24
Maple syrup, in Almond Milk Chai Martini, 87
Margarita Pitcher, Spicy Fantasy, 84
Marshmallows, in The Valkyries' Sleepover Grazing Board, 121–122
Martini, Almond Milk Chai, 87
Mascarpone, in The House's Double Chocolate Cake, 119–120
Mating Bond Lentil Soup, 54
Milk
　Almond Milk Chai Martini, 87
　Full Moon Black Sesame Pudding, 105
　Spicy Molten Chocolate, 91
　Thimblet Latte with Orange and Cardamom Espresso, 88
　Violet's Orange Creamsicle, 76
Mint Chocolate Lava Cupcakes, 109
Mint, fresh
　Calanmai Pomegranate Shakshuka, 20
　The Wing Leader's Pork Chop Meal, 70
Mozzarella cheese
　The Court of Dreams Appetizer: Caprese Skewers, 50
　Ruhn's Pizza: Pull-Apart Pizza Bread, 49
Mushrooms
　Aelin's Mushroom Onion Scramble, 19
　Cozy Beef Stew, 57
　Violet's Foraged Stuffed Mushrooms, 36
　Wendell's Mushroom Melt, 62

Noodles, Bryce's Chili, 61
Nuts. *See also* Almonds
　Full Moon Black Sesame Pudding, 105
　Roses and Thorns Apple Tartlets, 106
　The Valkyries' Sleepover Grazing Board, 121–122

Old fashioned oats, in A Warrior's Breakfast, 23
Orange juice
　Spicy Fantasy Margarita Pitcher, 84
　Violet's Orange Creamsicle, 76
Orange soda, in Violet's Orange Creamsicle, 76
Orange zest
　Thimblet Latte with Orange and Cardamom Espresso, 88
　A Warrior's Breakfast, 23
　Winter Solstice Ginger and Orange Pancakes, 10

Pancakes, Winter Solstice Ginger and Orange, 10
Parmesan cheese, in Mating Bond Lentil Soup, 54
Parsnips
　Autumn Equinox Pot Pie, 73
　Cozy Beef Stew, 57
　Feyre's First Fae Meal, 66
Pasta, in Bryce's Chili Noodles, 61
Pastry dough, in Autumn Equinox Pot Pie, 73. *See also* Puff pastry
Peanut butter
　Bryce's Chili Noodles, 61
　Dragon Breakfast Bowl, 24
Peas, in Autumn Equinox Pot Pie, 73
Pepitas, in Dragon Breath Spicy Chocolate Bark, 102
Pies, Savory Mini Meat, 46
Pizza Bread, Pull-Apart, 49
Poe's Glazed Cakes, 110
Pomegranate
　Blackberry and Bourbon Cauldron Punch, 80
　Calanmai Pomegranate Shakshuka, 20
Pork. *See also* Sausage
　Brennan's Honeyed Biscuit Breakfast Sandwiches, 15–16
　The Wing Leader's Pork Chop Meal, 70

INDEX

Porridge, in A Warrior's Breakfast, 23
Potatoes
  Autumn Equinox Pot Pie, 73
  Feyre's First Fae Meal, 66
Pot Pie, Autumn Equinox, 73
Pretzel rods, in The Valkyries' Sleepover Grazing Board, 121–122
Prosecco, in Faerie Wine Spritzer, 83
Pudding, Full Moon Black Sesame, 105
Puff pastry
  Cadet Breakfast Sausage Rolls, 27
  Roses and Thorns Apple Tartlets, 106
  Savory Mini Meat Pies, 46

Queen of Shadows (Maas), 19
Quinoa, in Fairy Bowl: Spring Vegetable Buddha Bowl, 58
Quite Large Cinnamon Buns, 113–114

Radishes
  Fairy Bowl: Spring Vegetable Buddha Bowl, 58
  Fairy Breakfast Savory Tart, 28
Red wine
  Cozy Beef Stew, 57
  Spiced Blood: Cranberry Sangria Punch, 79
Rice. *See* Wild rice
Rolls, in Lunathion Cedar-Smoked Grilled Cheeseburger Sliders, 45
Roma tomatoes
  Calanmai Pomegranate Shakshuka, 20
  Summer Court Ceviche, 35
Rosemary, fresh, in Feyre's First Fae Meal, 66
Roses and Thorns Apple Tartlets, 106
Ruhn's Pizza: Pull-Apart Pizza Bread, 49

Salami, in Fairy Charcuterie Board for Grazing, 39
Sandwiches
  The 33rd's Cafeteria Finger Sandwiches, 42
  Brennan's Honeyed Biscuit Breakfast Sandwiches, 15–16
  Lunathion Cedar-Smoked Grilled Cheeseburger Sliders, 45
  Wendell's Mushroom Melt, 62

Sausage
  Cadet Breakfast Sausage Rolls, 27
  Ruhn's Pizza: Pull-Apart Pizza Bread, 49
  A Warrior's Breakfast, 23
Savory Mini Meat Pies, 46
Sesame seeds, in Full Moon Black Sesame Pudding, 105
Shakshuka, Calanmai Pomegranate, 20
Shrimp, in Skull's Bay Spiced Prawns, 32
Simple syrup
  Blackberry and Bourbon Cauldron Punch, 80
  Spiced Blood: Cranberry Sangria Punch, 79
  Spicy Fantasy Margarita Pitcher, 84
  Thimblet Latte with Orange and Cardamom Espresso, 88
Skull's Bay Spiced Prawns, 32
Sliders, Lunathion Cedar-Smoked Grilled Cheeseburger, 45
Solstice Ginger and Orange Pancakes, 10
Soup, Mating Bond Lentil, 54
Sparkling water
  Blackberry and Bourbon Cauldron Punch, 80
  Spiced Blood: Cranberry Sangria Punch, 79
Spiced Blood: Cranberry Sangria Punch, 79
Spicy Fantasy Margarita Pitcher, 84
Spicy Molten Chocolate, 91
Spinach, in A Velaris Dinner: Lemon Verbena Swordfish, 65
Sprinkles, in The Valkyries' Sleepover Grazing Board, 121–122
Spritzer, Faerie Wine, 83
Squash, in Autumn Equinox Pot Pie, 73
Star anise, in Spiced Blood: Cranberry Sangria Punch, 79
Starlight Jam Linzer Cookies, 94
Sugar Cookies, Jasmine, 97
Summer Court Ceviche, 35

Tart, Fairy Breakfast Savory, 28
Tequila, in Spicy Fantasy Margarita Pitcher, 84

Thimblet Latte with Orange and Cardamom Espresso, 88
The 33rd's Cafeteria Finger Sandwiches, 42
Tomatoes, canned, in Calanmai Pomegranate Shakshuka, 20. *See also* Cherry tomatoes; Roma tomatoes
Trail mix, in Dragon Breakfast Bowl, 24
Truffles, Hibiscus, 101
Turkey, in The 33rd's Cafeteria Finger Sandwiches, 42

The Valkyries' Sleepover Grazing Board, 121–122
Vanilla wafer cookies, in The Valkyries' Sleepover Grazing Board, 121–122
A Velaris Dinner: Lemon Verbena Swordfish, 65
Violet's Foraged Stuffed Mushrooms, 36
Violet's Orange Creamsicle, 76

A Warrior's Breakfast, 23
Wendell's Mushroom Melt, 62
Werewolf Bowl: Steak and Wild Rice, 69
Whipped topping, in The Valkyries' Sleepover Grazing Board, 121–122
White wine
  Autumn Equinox Pot Pie, 73
  A Velaris Dinner: Lemon Verbena Swordfish, 65
Wild rice
  Mating Bond Lentil Soup, 54
  Werewolf Bowl: Steak and Wild Rice, 69
The Wing Leader's Pork Chop Meal, 70
Winter Solstice Ginger and Orange Pancakes, 10

Xaden's Mint Chocolate Lava Cupcakes, 109

Yarros, Rebecca, 15. *See also* Book titles/series by Rebecca Yarros
Yeast, in Quite Large Cinnamon Buns, 113–114